D1084847

Common
PRAYER

ALSO PUBLISHED
BY ONEWORLD

BY THE SAME AUTHOR

City of Wrong
The Event of the Qur'an
Jesus and the Muslim
Muhammad and the Christian

RELATED TITLES

The Faith and Practice of Al-Ghazálí, William
Montgomery Watt
Muslim Devotions, Constance E. Padwick
Muslims and Christians Face to Face, Kate Zebiri
What Muslims Believe, John Bowker

Common
PRAYER

*A Muslim–Christian
Spiritual Anthology*

Edited by KENNETH CRAGG

ONEWORLD
OXFORD

COMMON PRAYER

Oneworld Publications
(Sales and Editorial)
185 Banbury Road
Oxford OX2 7AR
England

Oneworld Publications
(US Marketing Office)
160 N Washington St.
4th floor, Boston
MA 02114, USA

Some of this material was previously published as
Alive to God, Oxford University Press, 1970

ISBN 1–85168–181–7

Cover and text design by Design Deluxe, Bath
Printed by CTPS, Hong Kong

The Editor's warm thanks go to Helen Coward of
Oneworld Publications for her meticulous care in
the production of this book.

CONTENTS

PREFACE

A PART IN COMMON PRAYER
DISCOVERED

'DISCUSSED' WILL follow in a postscript. Here, the preface can be brief, for the evidence is in the extracts that follow, namely a certain kinship of praise, penitence and petition from Muslim and Christian writings, a feasible fellowship, we might say, from Senegal to Samarkand.

There will be those who will greet the idea with doubt or hostility. How their misgivings, thoughtful or impulsive, might be overcome, their questions examined, can be deferred. Let the contents first be savoured and welcomed. Careful rationale may then seem unnecessary. However, for those in both faiths who are puzzled, even scandalized, by the bringing together of spiritualities so long deemed mutually exclusive, some careful reassurance is due. Having the evidence first may make the task less necessary. Hence the deliberate sequence here.

For it could be said that the anthology gathered itself. All that was needed was an eye for how far, and how often, sources in the two faiths proved a common territory. 'Common Prayer' in the making of the English Prayer Book in the sixteenth century (revised in the famous 1662 edition) meant 'Prayer in the vulgar tongue', no longer in the Latin few understood. To think of prayers 'common' through different theologies is a much more difficult matter than to move from Latin to English.

Perhaps this book should have been called *A Part in Common Prayer*. That title has five meanings. Only 'a part' of either community will be ready and willing participants. Only 'a part' of what they comprehend in faith and doctrine will be present. On both counts there will be no question of 'the whole'. In sharing they will be 'apart' from their full identity and – as is always true in praying – they will have 'come apart', as Jesus often bade his disciples, into quiet, seeking or, as the Qur'an puts it, 'desiring the face of God'.

The admitted partiality of the contents here has to be tested by reference in the postscript to the whole faith-identity of each religion. However, as partial it will be genuine. In the same context we must reckon with the many factors in contemporary life and society which require mutual response – response which has to reach back into the spiritual resources any faith can muster.

It should be clear that we are concerned not with formal ritual worship and the patterns of public liturgies obtaining in mosque and church, but rather with what Muslims know as *du'a'*, Christians as personal devotion. There is no merging here of those formal aptitudes which will always remain distinctive, with their sundry postures of kneeling, bowing, prostrating. Nevertheless, what here derives mainly from individual souls (Biblical and Quranic sources apart) may well serve in school assemblies, civic groups, or where people meet in – otherwise – only mental dialogue. Items grouped together have a certain unity and may suggest where independent thought might further go.

The Qur'an will be found more extensively quoted here than the New Testament. The reason, in part, is that the Qur'an, for Muslims, is primarily a recital. Memorizing the text, as is the tradition in Islam, means that Muslim mentality rides with its sequences and cadence. There is an immediacy in the verses, not merely as part *in* a whole, but part *for* a whole. Conversely, the index of authors shows more Christian sources than Muslim. This is because Christians, in literature and devotion, have taken livelier liberties than Muslims permit themselves.

Unaccredited prayers are by the compiler, as are the renderings of the Qur'an. Some items derive from non-believing sources, which is entirely right. Mystics and Sufis are represented, but this is not an anthology of Sufism. Were it such it would not be true to the breadth of Islam. A glance at the index indicates the range of enlistments, from close to twenty original languages and almost thirty countries. Senegal to Samarkand is no empty claim, thanks to President Senghor of the one and the Naqshabandi in the other. Each page makes its own point as users recognize, take, amend and pursue its hints and measures.

Let a discursive postscript take up what this brief introduction can well exclude. Demur can be the better faced when desire has had its way. Let necessary discussion bide its proper time. When George Herbert, the seventeenth-century English poet included here, tried to define prayer, he ventured some intriguing definitions, among them: 'God's breath in man returning to his birth', 'the soul in paraphrase' and 'a kind of tune'. He ended with the two words: 'Something understood'. He was cryptic but profound. Prayer must then mean 'Someone understood', and there our theologies differ in what they predicate of Allah. Yet not wholly so. In the 'Something' that prayer understands, in the intention and in the act, may be the part all praying parties share.

Kenneth Cragg
Oxford, 1999

THE SONG OF THE REED

Hearken to this reed forlorn,
Breathing ever since 'twas torn
From its rushy bed a strain
Of impassioned love and pain.

The secret of my song, though near,
None can see and none can hear.
O for a friend to know the sign
And mingle all his soul with mine!

'Tis the flame of love that fired me:
'Tis the wine of love inspired me.
Wouldst thou learn how lovers bleed?
Hearken, hearken to the reed.

JALAL AL-DIN RUMI: opening lines of his *Mathnawi*

PRAISE

O LORD God,
   inspire, determine and enable
      the intention of my life,
   that it be to thine honour.

Seal it as the desire of my heart,
   the purpose of my mind,
      the goal of my whole strength
   that it continue single, clear,
      immutable, importunate.

O Lord, be this intention, THOU:
   thy truth, thy work, thy love, thy glory.

Let it govern my words,
   dwell in my thoughts,
      purify my dealings,
         occupy and redeem my time.

Let it bring Thee into all my ways
   and the ways of those with whom I have to do,
      Thyself, thy light, thy salvation,
         thy wisdom, thy worship, thy blessing,
Today and always.

ERIC MILNER WHITE: *My God, My Glory*

SOMEONE SAID: 'Remember us in your intention. Intention is the root of the matter. If there be no words, let there be no words: words are the branch.'

JALAL AL-DIN RUMI: *Discourses*

To GOD belongs the praise, Lord of the heavens and Lord of the earth, the Lord of all being. His is the dominion in the heavens and in the earth: he is the Almighty, the All-wise.

Surah of the Kneeling 35

O THE DEPTH of the riches both of the wisdom and knowledge of God! How unsearchable are his judgments and his ways past finding out! For who hath known the mind of the Lord? Or who hath been his counsellor? Or who hath first given to him, and it shall be recompensed unto him again? For of him and through him and unto him are all things: to whom be glory for ever. Amen.

Epistle to the Romans 11.33–6

'TIS NO matter to amaze
If thy gifts outstripped my praise,
Or thy bounty overfilled
This my vessel, ere it spilled.

ABU-L-SALT: *Bounty*

GREAT AND marvellous are thy works, Lord God Almighty; just and true are thy ways, thou King of saints. Who shall not fear thee, O Lord, and glorify thy Name? For thou only art holy: for all nations shall come and worship before thee; for thy judgments are made manifest.

Book of Revelation 15.3–4

HE IS God. There is no god but he. He is the King, the only One, the Peace, the Trustworthy, the Preserver, the Almighty, the Ever-powerful, the Exalted.

Glory be to God beyond all that idolaters conceive.
He is God,
   Creator,
      Maker,
         Fashioner.
His are the most excellent Names.
All that is in the heavens and in the earth magnifies him, the Almighty, the Wise.

Surah of the Exile 23–4

GREAT ART thou, O Lord, and greatly to be praised. Great is thy power and thy wisdom is infinite. And thee would man praise, man but a particle of thy creation, man that bears about him his mortality, the witness of his sin, that thou resistest the proud. Yet would man praise thee, he but a particle of thy creation. Thou awakenest us to delight in thy praise. For thou madest us for thyself and our heart is restless until it rest in thee.

Grant me, Lord, to know and understand which is first – to call on thee or to praise thee? and again, to know thee or to call on thee? For who can call on thee, not knowing thee? For he that knoweth thee not may call on thee as other than thou art.

Or is it better that we call on thee that we may know thee?

AUGUSTINE OF HIPPO: opening lines of *Confessions*

NOW UNTO the King eternal, immortal, invisible, the only wise God, be honour and glory for ever, and ever. Amen.

First Epistle to Timothy 1.17

WHAT CAN I say to you, my God? Shall I collect together all the words that praise your holy Name? Shall I give you all the names of this world, you, the Unnameable? Shall I call you 'God of my life, meaning of my existence, hallowing of my acts, my journey's end, bitterness of my bitter hours, home of my loneliness, you my most treasured happiness'? Shall I say: Creator, Sustainer, Pardoner, Near One, Distant One, Incomprehensible One, God both of flowers and stars, God of the gentle wind and of terrible battles, Wisdom, Power, Loyalty and Truthfulness, Eternity and Infinity, you the All-merciful, you the Just One, you Love itself?

KARL RAHNER: *Prayers for Meditation*

IT IS God who made the earth for you as an abode and the heaven for a building. He fashioned you: comely did he fashion you and with good things did he provide you.

Blessed then be God your Lord, this God, Lord of all being. He is the living God: there is none save he.

Call upon him in sincerity of worship.

Praise be to God, the Lord of all being.

Surah of the Believers 66–7

O INFINITE God, Centre of my soul, convert me power-fully unto Thee.

THOMAS TRAHERNE: *Thanksgivings for the Body*

NONE MORE powerful is than he,
And yet how gracious is my Lord.
Of all 'mighties' known to men
He is the mightiest of them all.
How gracious is my Lord.

On none depends for any need,
To none in debt is he indeed,
He shaped the world in nothingness,
He is the Creator of one and all.
How gracious is my Lord.

Whatever is, he is the Maker,
Of earth and sky he is the builder:
Nothing concealed from him remains,
He sees and knoweth all that is.
How gracious is my Lord.

He is One with no compeer,
His oneness reflects his greatness.
He that hath his friendship
No other friend need seek.
How gracious is my Lord.

He is beginning and He the end,
He is changeless and eternal,
Rahman, gracious is my Lord.

RAHMAN BABA: *A Pushtu Poem*

HE IS the First and the Last.

Surah of Iron 3

HIS MERCY is on them that fear him, throughout all generations.

He hath put down the mighty from their seat, and exalted them of low degree.

He hath filled the hungry with good things; and as for the rich he sends them away empty.

The Gospel according to Luke 1.50, 52, 53

PRAISE BE to God, sovereign Lord, Author of the universe, who raises the winds and orders the morning, worshipped in religion and the Lord of the worlds. Praise be to God for his forbearance, when he knows all. Praise be to God for his pardon, though he is All-powerful. Praise be to God for his long-suffering in displeasure, though he is well able to do what he chooses.

Praise be to God, Lord of creation, Source of all livelihood, who orders the morning, Lord of majesty and honour, of grace and beneficence, He who is so far that he may not be seen and so near that he witnesses the secret things. Blessed be he and for ever exalted.

Praise be to God: he has no competitor to equal him and no peer to compare with him, and no helper to aid him. With his might he subdues the mighty and by his greatness the great are humbled. Whatever he wills by his power he attains.

Praise be to God who hearkens to me when I call upon him, covers my unworthiness when I have been rebellious and magnifies his grace upon me. I will not more transgress. I will sing to his praise and make mention of him in thanksgiving.

Ramadan Prayers

To thee be most high praise!
In worshipping thee we have not attained the fullness of
   worship,
O worshipped One.

To thee be most high praise!
In invoking thy Name we have not attained the fullness
   of invocation,
O thou who art invoked.

To thee be most high praise!
In thanking thee we have not attained unto the fullness
   of thanksgiving,
O Thou who art thanked.

To thee be most high praise!
In seeking thee we have not attained unto the fullness
   of seeking,
O thou who art the goal.

To thee be most high praise!
In describing thee we have not attained unto the
   fullness of description,
O thou who art described.

MUSTAFA AL-BAKRI: *Seal of the Five Prayers*

THOSE WHO attend permanently at the temple of his glory confess the imperfection of their worship and say: 'We have not worshipped thee according to the requirement of thy worship': and those who describe the splendour of his beauty are rapt in amazement saying: 'We have not known thee as thou oughtest to be known.'

SA'DI: *The Gulistan*

WE HAVE set in the heavens constellations making them glorious to behold . . . and the earth we have stretched out, whereon are borne the great mountains and where we have caused everything to grow accordingly, providing there a livelihood for you and for those for whom you take no liability. There is nothing whose treasure sources are not ours, and all are constituted from above in their appointed measure. We send the fertilizing winds and bring down the rain from heaven, giving you to drink of reservoirs that are not yours.

Surah of al-Hijr 16, 19–22

O ALL ye works of the Lord, bless ye the Lord,
　Praise him and magnify him for ever.

O ye mountains and hills, bless ye the Lord,
　Praise him and magnify him for ever.

O all ye green things upon the earth, bless ye the Lord,
　Praise him and magnify him for ever.

O ye children of men, bless ye the Lord,
　Praise him and magnify him for ever.

O ye servants of the Lord, bless ye the Lord,
　Praise him and magnify him for ever.

O ye spirits and souls of the righteous, bless ye the Lord,
　Praise him and magnify him for ever.

O ye holy and humble men of heart, bless ye the Lord,
　Praise him and magnify him for ever.

Benedicite Omnia Opera

To GOD belong the east and the west and wheresoever you turn there is the Face of God. Truly God is All-pervading, All-knowing.

Surah of the Cow 115

LO! GOD is here, let us adore
    And own how dreadful is this place:
Let all within us feel his power
    And silent bow before his face:
Who know his power, his grace who prove,
    Serve him with fear, with reverence love.

Lo! God is here, him day and night
    The united choirs of angels sing:
To him, enthroned above all height,
    Heaven's hosts their noblest praises bring.
To him may all our thoughts arise,
    In never ceasing sacrifice.

GERHARDT TERSTEEGEN, translated by John Wesley

I HAVE only one desire
To feel you close beside me,
As did Moses on the peak of Sinai.

AMIR HAMZAH: *One Alone*

IN THE Name of God upon my heart
    That its thirst may be quenched.

In the Name of God upon my knees
    That they may be strengthened.

In the Name of God upon the earth,
    That it may be traversed.

'ABD AL-QADIR AL-JILANI: *Wells of Prayer*

I ASKED THE earth and it answered me: 'I am not it' and all things whatsoever in it made the same confession. I asked the sea and the deeps and the creeping things and they answered me: 'We are not thy God; seek beyond us . . .' I asked the heavens, the sun and moon and stars: 'Nor', say they, 'are we the God thou seekest.'

AUGUSTINE OF HIPPO: *Confessions*

A CCORDINGLY, WE showed Abraham the kingdom of the heavens and of the earth, that he might be one of sure faith. As night darkened round him he beheld a star and said: 'This is my Lord.' But when it set, he said: 'I cannot love what sets.' And when he saw the moon rising he said: 'This is my Lord.' But when it set he said: 'If my Lord does not guide me aright, I shall surely be among the erring.'

And when he saw the sun rising he said: 'This is my Lord; this is greater.' But when it also set he said: 'O my people, I have finished with all your idolatrous things. As for me, my face is towards the One who created the heavens and the earth, as a man of pure faith. I am not a worshipper of false deities.'

Surah of Cattle 75–9

GLORY BE to thee, O Lord, glory be to thee.
    Creator of the visible light,
        the sun's ray, the flame of fire.
Creator also of the light invisible and intellectual,
    that which is known to God,
            writings of the law, oracles of the prophets,
            melody of psalms, instruction of proverbs,
            experience of histories,
            a light that never sets.
God is the Lord, who has showed us light.

LANCELOT ANDREWES: *Preces Privatae*

YOU SET up the sky like a canopy and spread it out like a tent. By a mere act of will you gave the earth stability when there was nothing to uphold it. You established the firmament . . . and set in order the chorus of the stars to praise your magnificence.

Prayer at the Eucharist: Apostolic Constitutions

WHICH WAS the harder task in creating, you or the heaven he reared? He raised the canopy of heaven and set it in poise. He made the night a cover over it and he brought forth its high noon. And then he laid the expanse of the earth, bringing forth waters and pastures therein, and he made fast the hills to be a joy to you and to your flocks.

Surah of the Spoilers 27–31

O GOD, I call upon thee by thy great truth, by the truth of the light of thy gracious countenance, the truth of thy mighty throne, by that greatness and majesty, beauty and splendour, power and authority, of thine that uphold thy throne, and by the reality of thy Names, hidden and concealed, which none of thy creatures has pondered.

O God, I call upon thee by the Name that thou has set upon the night that it became dark, and upon the day that it became light, upon the heavens that they spread forth, and upon the earth that it came to rest, upon the mountains that they stood, and upon the seas and valleys that they flow, upon the fountains that they rise and the clouds that they give rain.

Prayers of the Naqshabandi Order

PRAISE BE to him who alone is to be praised. Praise him for his grace and favour. Praise him for his power and goodness. Praise him whose knowledge encompasses all things.

'O God, grant me light in my heart and light in my tomb, light in my hearing and light in my seeing, light in my hair and light in my skin, light in my flesh and light in my blood and light in my bones.

Light before me, light behind me, light to right of me, light to left of me, light above me, light beneath me.

O God, increase my light and give me the greatest light of all. Of thy mercy grant me light, O thou most merciful.'

ABU HAMID AL-GHAZALI: *The Beginning of Guidance*

OPEN THOU mine eyes and I shall see:
Incline my heart and I shall desire:
Order my steps and I shall walk
In the ways of thy commandments.

O Lord God, be thou to me a God
And beside thee let there be none else,
No other, nought else with Thee.

Vouchsafe to me to worship thee and serve thee
According to thy commandments,
   In truth of spirit,
     In reverence of body,
       In blessing of lips,
         In private and in public,
To overcome evil with good.

LANCELOT ANDREWES: *Preces Privatae*

EVERYTHING WITH him has its measure, Knower of the unseen and of the seen, All-great and All-exalted: it is all the same with him whether your word is furtive or open loud, whether you go stealthily in the night or fare forth in the open day.

Surah of Thunder 9–10

O GOD, ALL-POWERFUL, true and incomparable, present in all things, yet limited by none, uncircumscribed by place, unaged by time, unhurried by the years, not beguiled by words, not subject to birth, never in need of protection, far above corruption, admitting of no change, by nature immutable, living in light that none can approach, essentially invisible, yet known to all rational beings that ponder on thee lovingly and grasped by those who seek thee because thou art dear to them . . .

Deal with us after thy lovingkindness . . . Bless these people whose heads are bowed before thee . . . make them holy, watch over them, protect them and support them, deliver them from the adversary and all other enemies, guard them in their going out and their coming in.

To thee be all praise, glory, greatness, adoration and worship . . . for ever, age upon age.

Final blessing in the Eucharist: Apostolic Constitutions

VOUCHSAFE TO me
A Scroll, I pray
My shield to be
In fate's affray.

Let your right hand
Inscribe thereon:
'Praise God most High,
Praise him alone.'

HAFSA OF GRANADA: *The Shield*

MY GOD, I love thee thyself above all else and thee I desire as my last end. Always and in all things, with my whole strength and heart and with unceasing labour, I seek thee. If thou give not thyself to me thou givest nothing. If I find thee not I find nothing. Grant to me, therefore, most loving God, that I may ever love thee for thyself above all things in this life present, so that at last I may find thee and keep thee for ever in the world to come.

THOMAS BRADWARDINE

O GOD, WHO art rich and praiseworthy, who createst and restorest to life, who art merciful and loving, make me to abound in what is lawful in thy sight, in obedience to thee and by grace from thee, so that I turn from what is unlawful, from disobedience and from all other than thou.

ABU HAMID AL-GHAZALI: *The Beginning of Guidance*

ON YOU we call, Lord God,
All-wise, All-surveying, All-holy,
The only true Sovereign.

You created the universe:
You watch over all that exists.
Those who lie in darkness,
Overshadowed by death,
You guide into the right road, the safe road.
Your will is that all men should be saved
And come to the knowledge of the truth.

With one voice we offer you
Praise and thanksgiving.

Egyptian Christian papyrus: Patrologia Latina

BY THE manifestation of thy surpassing glory, bring me out of every kind of ignorant neglect, wherein I might lose thee at any breath of mine or moment of time. Show to me thy nature as light, lifting off the shadows of mortal being that I may be among the companions of the Face.

To thee, O my God, is the rising and the setting sun: at every turn there is the Face of God.

AHMAD IBN IDRIS: *Prayers*

ADDRESSING ALL well-meaning but unmortified men, wandering aimlessly on the paths of self-love and finding no consolation either in God or creatures, because their hearts are thrown about from one confusion to another, I invite them to turn their backs on the stifling vanities of self-absorption. *Sursum corda:* lift up your hearts.

HENRY SUSO: *The Exemplar*

HOW EXCELLENT is thy lovingkindness, O God.
We commend to thee, Lord, our impulses and our
    incentives,
Our intentions and our ventures,
Our going out and our coming in,
Our sitting down and our rising up.
How truly, meet, and right, and comely, and due,
    In all and for all,
    In all places, times and manners,
    In every season, every spot,
    Everywhere, always, altogether,
To remember thee, to worship thee,
To confess to thee, to praise thee,
To bless thee, to give thanks to thee,
    Maker, Nourisher, Guardian, Governor,
    Healer, Benefactor, Protector of all.

LANCELOT ANDREWES: *Preces Privatae*

PRAISE BE to God who feeds us and give us to drink, who suffices for us and shelters us. How many there are who have none to be to them either sufficiency or haven. In thy Name, O God, I live and in thy Name I die.

O Lord, I ask of thee, from thy Presence, a mercy by which thou wilt guide my heart and order my concern, a mercy by which thou wilt repair my distractedness and bring back my alertness, a mercy cleansing my works and inspiring my ways, a mercy ennobling what I mean to others and reuniting me with those to whom I belong, a mercy whereby thou preservest me from every evil.

This, O God, is my prayer. Thine it is to hear. This is my yearning. On thee is all my reliance.

Prayer of the Prophet Muhammad according to Abu Hamid al-Ghazali

By THE sun and the midday glory
And the moon that follows after.
By the day telling its splendour
And the night that envelops it.
By the heaven and its rearing,
By the earth and its shaping,
By the soul and its ensouling.

Surah of the Sun 1–7

ALL THAT is in the heavens and in the earth magnifies God: for he is Almighty and All-wise. To him belong the kingdoms of the heavens and of the earth, and unto God is the returning of all things. He makes the night to give way to the day, and the day to the night, and he knows the innermost hearts.

Surah of Iron 1, 5–6

Awake my glory, my lute and harp myself shall wake.
Soon as the stately, night-exploding bird,
In lively lay, sings welcome to the dawn.
List ye! how nature with ten thousand tongues,
Begins the glad thanksgiving.
All hail! ye tenants of the forest and the field,
My fellow subjects of the eternal King,
    I gladly join your matins and with you
    Confess his Presence and report his praise.
O thou, who or the lambkin or the dove,
When offered by the lowly, meek and poor,
Preferest to pride's hecatomb,
Accept this mean essay,
Nor from thy treasure-house of glory immense
The orphan's mite exclude.

O could I search the bosom of the sea,
Down the great deeps descending, there thy works
Would also speak thy residence: and there
Would I, thy servant, like the still profound,
Astonished into silence, muse thy praise.
Vain were the attempt, and impious, to trace
Through all his works the Artificer Divine,
And though no shining sun, nor twinkling star
Bedecked the crimson curtain of the sky,
Yet man, at home within himself, might find

The Deity immense, and in that frame,
So fearfully, so wonderfully, made
    See and adore his providence and power . . .
The knee which thou hast shaped shall bend to thee,
The tongue which thou hast tuned shall chant thy praise,
And thine own image, the immortal soul,
Shall consecrate herself to thee for ever.

CHRISTOPHER SMART: *Awake my Glory*

'L IFT UP your hearts!'
Whenever I say the words: *Sursum corda!* my heart and soul seem to be melting away with Divine love and compassion . . . Reflections set my heart on fire and spread out their hungry flames to ignite the heart of all animate creatures. Sometimes they occur to me singly, sometimes all together. First, I contemplate in spirit all my being, my soul, my body and all my powers, and place all the creatures with which God has peopled the earth, the heavens and the elements.

Next, I consider creatures individually: the birds of the air, the beasts of the forest, the fish in the waters, the plants of the earth, the sands of the seashore, the tiny cobwebs in each ray of sunshine, the snowflakes, raindrops and dewy diamonds, and reflect that each of these creatures obeys God, thus contributing to the mysterious concord of sweet sounds which ascends to the Creator as an unceasing *Te Deum* in praise of his mercy. Then I imagine myself as choirmaster directing this mystical chorus, and I invite and prompt all the members to uplift their hearts and souls to God: *Sursum corda!*

HENRY SUSO: *The Exemplar*

I T IS he who made the sun a splendour and the moon a light, ordaining its phases that you might register the years and make reckoning. He created them with truth alone, distinguishing the signs to men of understanding. Surely in the alternation of day and night and through all God's creation in the heavens and in the earth are signs for those who fear him.

Surah of Jonah 5–6

I CONSIDER MY own heart and those of all men and reflect on the joy, love and peace of those who consecrate all their faculties to God's service and the contrasting misery, bitterness, and unrest with which the world repays her devotees. Then I invite all men living on earth to join me in the zealous service of God, saying: 'O poor, imprisoned human hearts, lift yourself above the walls which enclose you! Wake up, sleeping hearts, throw aside the apathy of your sluggish, careless habits. Take flight heavenwards on the wings of a true and complete conversion to the God of all love. Lift up your hearts!'

HENRY SUSO: *The Exemplar*

T HY NAME be glorified for evermore for all the art which thou hast hidden in this little piece of red clay.
For the workmanship of thy hand, who didst form man of the dust of the ground, and breathe into his nostrils the breath of life.
Thy works speaking to me the same thing that was said unto Adam in the beginning: 'We are all thine.'

Even for our earthly bodies thou hast created all things: the influences of heaven,
    Clouds, vapours, winds, dew, rain, hail, snow,
      Light and darkness, night and day,
    The seasons of the year, springs, rivers, fountains,
      Corn, wine and oil, the sun, moon and stars,
    Cities, nations, kingdoms,
      And the bodies of men, the greatest treasures of all,
    For each other.

THOMAS TRAHERNE: *Thanksgivings for the Body*

O THOU ON whose generosity and the beauty of thy customs all petitioners depend, praise be to thee.

'ABD AL-QADIR AL-JILANI: *Wells of Prayer*

HAVE THEY not beheld the heaven above them? How we established and adorned it in its unbroken reach? And the earth also we stretched out and set thereon the mighty hills, where we made every kind of joyous thing to grow, for insight and for token to every penitent servant. And from heaven we have sent down the blessed rain whereby we make the gardens grow, and grain of harvest and tall palm trees laden with clustered dates, in provision for men, thereby bringing again to life a land that was dead – similitude of 'the coming forth'.

Surah Qaf 6–11

BE PRESENT, merciful Lord, with us thy creatures that our joy in thy creation may kindle into true thanksgiving and season all our dealings in house and market, in producing and consuming. Let the sense of thy bounty hallow our thoughts and our exchanges, for the doing of thy will and the glory of thy Name. Amen.

LOVE CAME a guest
Within my breast,
My soul was spread,
Love banqueted.

IBN HAZM: *The Ring of the Dove*

D o you not see that God it is whom all things praise in the heavens and in the earth and the birds too on wings of flight? Each truly knows its prayer and its praising and God knows their every deed.

For to God belongs the kingdom of the heavens and of the earth and unto him is their becoming.

Surah of Light 41–2

THY BEAUTY shines O God, through all created things
In all this wide, immeasurable universe,
Thou art expressed, revealed,
Brought close and intimate and near.

Thy love, most mighty and most sweet,
In song of birds, in sunset clouds,
In flower, in wind and star,
Is eloquent and tangible and close.

Ungainly, foolish words!
How can mere words,
The mask and darkening of reality,
Express thy Being?
How can mere words
Set forth thy praise?

JOHN S. HOYLAND: *The Fourfold Sacrament*

I HOLD the splendid daylight in my hands . . .
Daylight like a fine fan spread from my hands,
Daylight like scarlet poinsettias,
Daylight like yellow cassia flowers,
Daylight like clean water,
Daylight like green cacti,
Daylight like sea sparkling with white horses,
Daylight like tropic hills,
Daylight like a sacrament in my hands.

GEORGE CAMPBELL: *Litany*

WALK WITH thy fellow-creatures: note the bush
And whispers amongst them. There's not a spring,
Or leaf but hath his morning hymn: each bush
And oak doth know I AM: canst thou not sing?

When seasons change then lay before thine eye
His wondrous method: mark the various scenes
In heav'n: hail, thunder, rainbow, snows and ice,
Calms, tempests, lights and darkness by His means:
Thou canst not miss His praise. Each tree, herb, flower
Are shadows of His wisdom and His power.

HENRY VAUGHAN: *Rules and Lessons*

THE KINGDOM is his: there is no god but he. Why, then, are you alienated? Though you deny the faith, God is altogether rich without you. Yet he takes no pleasure in unfaith, ingratitude on the part of his servants, he delights in you in your thankfulness.

Surah of Thunder 6–7

WHAT BOUND may we assign,
O God, to any work of Thine!
Their endlessness discovers Thee
    In all to be divine:
        A Deity,
That will for evermore exceed the end
Of all that creature's wit can comprehend.

Thy soul, O God, doth prize
The seas, the earth, our souls, the skies,
As we return the same to Thee
    They more delight Thine eyes
        And sweeter be
As unto Thee we offer up the same,
Than as to us from Thee at first they came.

THOMAS TRAHERNE: *Amendment*

O THOU whose power o'er moving worlds presides,
Whose voice created and whose wisdom guides,
On darkling man in pure effulgence shine
And cheer the clouded mind with light divine.

'Tis Thine alone to calm the pious breast
With silent confidence and holy rest.
From Thee, great God, we spring, to Thee we tend,
Path, motive, guide, original and friend.

BOETHIUS: *On the Consolations of Philosophy*,
versified by Samuel Johnson

'TIS THINE without reserve, most simply thine,
So given to thee that it is not my own
A willing captive of thy grace divine
And loves and seeks thee for thyself alone.

'Tis all thine own: my spirit is so too
An undivided offering at thy shrine.
It seeks thy glory with no double view,
Thy glory with no secret bent to mine.

But I am silent, seeing what I see –
And fear, with cause, that I am self-deceived.
Not even my faith is from suspicion free
And that I love seems not to be believed.

WILLIAM COWPER: *Poetical Works*

RUMOUR OF the fierce-pulsed city far way
Breaks upon peace that aureoles our rest,
Shut the eyes that flame and hush the heart that burns.
God gives wisdom to the spirit that upturns.
Let us adore now, you and I.

GEORGE W. RUSSELL: *Prayer*

IN MY weakness, Lord, make perfect Thine own strength. Amen.

MY GOD and my Lord, eyes are at rest, stars are setting,
hushed are the movements of birds in their nests, of
monsters in the deep.
And thou art the just who knowest no change, the equity
that swerveth not, the everlasting that passeth not away.
The doors are locked, watched by their bodyguards.
But thy door is open to him who calls on thee.
My Lord, each lover is now alone with his beloved.
Thou for me art the beloved One.

'ABD AL-'AZIZ AL-DIRINI: *Purity of Heart*

. . . TO SEE
Mortals subdued in all the shapes of sleep.
Here lay two sister twins in infancy:
There, a lone youth who in his dreams did weep:
Within, two lovers linked innocently
In their loose locks, which over both did creep
Like ivy from one stem: and there lay calm
Old age with snow-bright hair and folded palm.

But other troubled forms of sleep she saw,
Not to be mirrored in a holy song –
Distortions foul of supernatural awe
And pale imaginings of visioned wrong,
And all the code of custom's lawless law,
Written upon the brows of old and young.

PERCY B. SHELLEY: *The Witch of Atlas*

LIGHTEN OUR darkness, we beseech thee, O Lord, and by
thy great mercy defend us from all perils and dangers
of this night.

The Book of Common Prayer

To him belongs whatsoever inhabits the day and the night.

Surah of Cattle 13

About him all the sanctities of heaven
Stood thick as stars and from his sight receiv'd
Beatitude past utterance.

John Milton: *Paradise Lost*

The duteous day now closeth,
Each flower and tree reposeth,
Shade creeps o'er wild and wood.
   Let us, as night is falling,
    On God, Our Maker calling,
Give thanks to him the Giver good.

Now all the heavenly splendour
Breaks forth in starlight tender
From myriad worlds unknown.
   And man the marvel seeing,
    Forgets his selfish being
For joy of beauty not his own.

Awhile his mortal blindness
May miss God's lovingkindness
And grope in faithless strife.
   But when life's day is over
    Shall death's fair night discover
The fields of everlasting life.

Paulus Gerhardt: *Hymn at Nightfall*

ALL THINGS suppliant unto thee are beloved of thee. O God, I call upon thee by thy majesty at its most radiant, for every splendour of thine is truly splendid.

Ramadan Prayers

LET MAN ponder over the food he eats: how we poured down rains abundantly and opened up the earth, making grain to grow therein and grapes and green fodder and olive trees and date palms and thickly bearing orchards, fruits and pastures, providing for you and for your flocks.

Surah 'He Frowned' 24–32

LORD GOD, out of your kindness to men, bless the fruits you have given us and bless your servants gathered for the work of harvest. Grant salvation also to those who possess these fruits that, having the abundance that comes from you, they may show to the poor the kindness that is also yours. To that end accept our whole worship.

Patrologia Orientalis

O LORD GOD, whose compassions fail not, grant us grace so to recognize and receive thy mercies that we may fashion our own selves after the same pattern of kindliness and care, for the praise of thy great Name. Amen.

Bless, O Lord, we pray thee, our taking of bread and let it be in our dependence, for gratefulness; of our community, for sign; and in our using, for comfort and strength; and thine be the praise this day and always. Amen.

O Lord, who has taught us to acknowledge in daily bread a debt to our fellows, known and unknown, grant us in the strength thereof to live in truly human bonds of compassion, for thy truth and thy love's sake. Amen.

O THOU WHOSE beauty no thoughts can encompass.
O thou whose perfection no vision can conceive.

Invocations from Hirz al-Jawshan

SPRING LEAVES upon the emerald plain
Embroideries of green again . . .
Again the daffodils have spun
Their dances with the wind and sun.
Anemones the rivals are
Of roses that bedeck the car
Of state, the roses hang their head
And glow more sorrowfully red:
Whereas the lily doth unite
Within herself all heaven's light.

ABU-L-'ALA AL-MA'ARI: *Poems*

WHAT WOULD Heaven and Earth be worth, were there
no spectator, no enjoyer? As much, therefore, as
the end is better than the means, the thought of the
world whereby it is enjoyed is better than the world . . . The
world within you is an offering returned, which is infinitely
more acceptable to God Almighty, since it came from him
that it might return unto him.

Wherein the mystery is great. For God hath made you
able . . . to give and offer up the world unto him, which is
very delightful in flowing from him, but much more in
returning to him . . . Let all your actions proceed from a
sense of this greatness, let all your affections extend to this
infinite wideness . . . and let all your praises arise and ascend
from this fountain.

THOMAS TRAHERNE: *Centuries of Meditations*

HE MADE the confluence of the two waters and the bound between them which they may not pass.

Surah of Al-Rahman 19–20

THE MOVING waters at their priestlike task
Of pure ablution round earth's human shores.

JOHN KEATS: *Sonnet, Bright Star*

AS THE inhastening tide doth roll,
Home from the deep, along the whole
Wide shining strand, and floods the caves –
Your love comes filling with happy waves
The open seashore of my soul.

ALICE MEYNELL: *The Visiting Sea*

CORRUPTION IS evident on land and sea by the deeds of men's hands and he has made them taste, in part, the entail of their deeds so that perhaps they may turn again.

Surah of the Byzantines 41

LORD OF the welcoming shore, the reassuring beach, the harbour where the waves are stilled, praise be to thee for firm terrain and guardian cliffs that hold the tides in place. Praise be to thee for the cycle-course of sun and cloud returning from the salt the springs and streams of the benign waters that yield the crops and fruits of the ever-bearing earth. Be thou, O Lord, our theme of human praise from land and sea. Amen.

I SAY, TOO, that the admiration we feel at works of crafts-manship is akin to the wonder we feel at the works of nature. For what craftsmanship produces is from one point of view a work of nature, inasmuch as it is effectuated by dint of natural forces. Thus the engineer is worthy of our praise who succeeds in moving a heavy weight: but would he not have much greater claim on our admiration if he could make a model capable of handling any weight at all? 'It is God who has created both you and all you do.' Blessed, then, be he whose dominion extends through both the worlds of the visible and the invisible and within your own selves also. Do you not comprehend? The light of his majesty shines forth and no veil can overcome it. He knows that which eludes the eye and what is hidden in the heart. For all that exists is by his power alone and is in motion or at rest according to his will. The fulfilment of his will is all their joy and drawing near to his holy presence is their great delight. By their multiplicity they witness to his unity and by their very changes they confess his abidingness. There is nothing that does not celebrate his praise.

'ABD AL-LATIF AL-BAGHDADI: *The Book of Instruction*

AND SO to God, Eternal Lord, Master of creation, Maker and Ruler of men,

Be the glory and the praise,

> from the wonder of our senses,
> from the skill of our hands,
> from the powers in our ordering,
> from the purpose of our being,
> from the offering of our worship,

To him be the dominion in all things everywhere. Amen.

ONLY THE face of your Lord abides in majesty and glory all his own.

Surah of Al-Rahman 27

MY HEART prepar'd, prepared is my heart
    To spread Thy praise
    With tuned lays:
  Wake my tongue, my lute awake,
  Thou my heart the consort make,
My self will bear a part.

My self when first the morning shall appear,
    With voice and string
    So will Thee sing:
  That this earthly globe, and all
  Treading on this earthly ball
My praising notes shall hear.

For God, my only God, Thy gracious love
    Is mounted far
    Above each star,
  Thy unchanged verity
  Heav'nly wings do lift as high
As clouds have room to move.

As high as highest heav'n can give Thee place
    O Lord ascend
    And thence extend
  With most bright, most glorious show
  Over all the earth below,
The sunbeams of Thy face.

MARY, COUNTESS OF PEMBROKE: Miserere mei, Deus

FOR LOVE of him they give food to the destitute, the orphan and the captive. 'We feed you,' they say, 'mindful only of the face of God. We want neither reward nor thanks on your part. We stand in fear of the Day of our Lord!'

Surah of Man 8–10

PENITENCE

O THOU who acceptest penitent acts.

Thou who art greatly beneficent.

Thou who hearkenest unto those who call.

Thou who knowest hidden things.

O thou before whose greatness everything is humbled.

O thou before whom everything bows in awe.

O thou by whose command the heavens and the earth abide.

O thou in whose fear all things obey.

Thou goal of all hopes: thou refuge of every outcast.

O Master of the covenant and promise.

O thou who bestowest our requests.

O thou who discoverest the distress of every weary soul.

O thou who concealest every blemished thing.

O thou companion of every lonely soul.

O thou who befriendest me in my solitariness.

O thou who companionest me in my loneliness.

O thou who art faithful in covenant.

O thou who bestowest our desires.

O Lord of majesty and power.

Invocations from Hirz al-Jawshan

O GOD, MY only plea is my plight, all I have to offer is my lack. My intercessor is my tears, my treasure is my frailty.

O my God, a drop from the ocean of your glory will suffice me. Have mercy upon me, provide me, pardon me and it will be pardoned me. Breathe on my sorrow and make glad my stress and strain by your mercy, the ever All-Merciful.

'ABD AL-'AZIZ AL-DIRINI: *Taharat al-Qulub*

O MY GOD, how can you recoil back upon us our sins – we in our poverty yearning after what befits you? We who have repaired to your door, take us into your pity with your beloved ones.

It is the utmost grace to us that we should be your servants: it suffices us for honour that you should be our Lord.

O my God, you are to us in the measure of your love, make us to be yours by that measure of our being loved.

O my God, all joy save with you fades away, all employ save yours is empty. To rejoice in you is joy indeed, while happiness without you deludes.

'ABD AL-'AZIZ AL-DIRINI: *Taharat al-Qulub*

WILT THOU not yield me vision,
Lord of grace,
Of that vast realm
Of unhorizoned space
Which is Thy heart
That heart-room makes for all?

Hebridean Altars

THE MIND of man, as it must be stirred up in the morning, so must it also in the evening, as by a note of recall. It is called back to itself and to its Leader by a scrutiny of self, by prayers and thanksgivings.

There are many hiding places and recesses in the mind. The heart is deceitful above all things. The old man is bound up in a thousand folds. Therefore, take heed to thyself . . . We think him not safe who is undefended by the arms and guard of prayer.

LANCELOT ANDREWES: *Preces Privatae*

O OUR LORD, take us not to task, if we forget or miss the mark. O our Lord, lay not on us a burden like that which thou didst lay on those before us. O our Lord, lay not on us that which we have no strength to carry. Pardon and forgive us. Thou art our Master.

Surah of the Cow 286

HAVE MERCY upon us.
Have mercy upon our efforts, that we
Before thee, in love and in faith,
Righteousness and humility,
May follow thee, with self-denial,
Steadfastness and courage,
And meet thee in silence.

Give us a pure heart that we may see thee,
A humble heart that we may hear thee,
A heart of love that we may serve thee,
A heart of faith that we may live thee.

DAG HAMMARSKJÖLD: *Markings*

H E KNOWS the treachery of the eyes and what the breasts conceal.

Surah of the Believers 19

I LOOKED AT myself as I then was. Worldly interests encompassed me on every side . . . When I considered the intention of my teaching, I perceived that instead of doing it for God's sake alone I had no active motive but the desire for glory and reputation. I realized that I stood on the edge of a precipice.

ABU HAMID AL-GHAZALI: *The Deliverer from Wandering*

WITH 'No Admittance' printed on my heart
I go abroad and play my public part and
Win applause. I have no cause to be
Ashamed of that strange self that others see.

But how can I reveal, to you, and you,
My real self's hidden and unlovely hue?
How can I un-deceive, how end despair
Of this intolerable make-believe?

You must see with God's eyes, or I must wear
My furtive failures stark upon my sleeve.

BASIL DOWLING: *Signs and Wonders*

A LMIGHTY GOD, unto whom all hearts are open, all desires known, and from whom no secrets are hid: cleanse the thoughts of our hearts by the inspiration of thy Holy Spirit, that we may perfectly love thee and worthily magnify thy holy Name.

The Book of Common Prayer

LORD, THOU knowest that I am a hundred hundred times worse than thou has declared. But beyond my exertion and action, beyond good and evil, faith and infidelity, beyond living righteously or behaving disobediently, I had great hope of thy lovingkindness. I turn again to that pure grace. I am not regarding my own works. Thou gavest me my being as a robe of honour: I have always relied on that munificence.

JALAL AL-DIN RUMI: *The Man who Looked Back on his Way to Hell*

O GOD, I am ashamed to lift up my face to thee.
  For I have done evil in thy sight,
  Not keeping thy commandments,
  Not doing thy will,
And now my heart kneels to thee,
  Beseeching thy goodness.

I have sinned, O Lord, I have sinned,
  And know my iniquities.
  I pray thee, remit to me, remit to me,
Nor reserve evil for me, nor condemn me.

For thou art God, the God of penitents.
  Show in me all thy lovingkindness,
  And save me, though unworthy,
For thy great mercy.

Let thy tender mercies speedily prevent us,
  For we are brought very low.
  Deliver us and purge away our sins,
For thy Name's sake.

LANCELOT ANDREWES: *Preces Privatae*

O MY GOD, how gentle art thou with him who has transgressed against thee: how near thou art to him who seeks thee, how tender to him who petitions thee, how kindly to him who hopes in thee.

Who is he who asked of thee and thou didst deny him, or who sought refuge in thee and thou didst betray him, or drew near to thee and thou didst hold him aloof, or fled unto thee and thou didst repulse him?

Thine, O Lord, is the creation and the authority.

By what is hidden of thy Names and by what the veils conceal of thy splendour, forgive this restless soul, this anguished heart.

O God, we seek in thee refuge from all abasement save unto thee: from all fear save thine: from all poverty save with thee.

O God, as thou hast kept our faces from prostration to any save thee, so keep our hands from being stretched out in petition to any save thee. For there is no god but thee.

Verily I was among the wrongdoers. But praise be to God, the Lord of the worlds.

Prayers of the Naqshabandi Order

PRAISE BE to God. O God, thou art the One to whom we give thanks. I pray the Lord to forgive us for those things which we have done and those things which we shall do in the future. Lord God, drive away from us all sorrow and the envy of enemies, and deliver us from the evil of this world and the next.

ABUBAKAR TAFAWA BALEWA: *Shaihu Umar*

O GOD, THOU hast many claims on me for what is between me and thee, and there are many claims against me in my relation to the world of thy creation.

O God, release me of that owed to thee and bear for me that which is between me and thy creation.

Pilgrimage Prayers

GOD IN heaven,
Let me really feel my nothingness,
Not in order to despair over it,
But in order to feel the more powerfully
The greatness of thy goodness.

SØREN KIERKEGAARD: *Journals*

O LORD GOD, thou knowest my secret and my open things: Receive my plea. Thou knowest my need. Grant, therefore, my petition. Thou knowest all that is in my soul.

O Lord God, I ask of thee a faith to occupy my heart and a true assurance, whereby I may know that nought shall ever befall me outside thy purposed will for me. Let me be well pleased with whatever thou allottest me, O thou Lord of majesty and honour.

ABU HAMID AL-GHAZALI: *The Reviving of Religion,* 'Prayer of Adam'

ALMIGHTY . . .
Forgive my doubt, my anger, my pride.
By thy mercy abase me,
By thy strictness raise me up.

DAG HAMMARSKJÖLD: *Markings*

BE CLOTHED with humility: for God resisteth the proud and giveth grace to the humble. Humble yourselves, then, under the mighty hand of God, that in due time he may exalt you, casting all your care upon him: for he cares for you.

First Epistle of Peter 5.5–7

OGOD, PRESERVE me from evil allurements and keep me from all tribulations. Make good both my inward and my outward man and cleanse my heart from hatred and envy. Let not any man have any issue against me.

O God, I seek of thee to lay hold of the good and to forsake the evil, as thou knowest them. Undertake, I pray thee, for my protection and give me simplicity in my living and by clear guidance a way out of all dubiety and victory with the right in every argument.

Grant me to be just, both in anger and in good pleasure and submissive to what the decree brings. Make me moderate both in poverty and wealth, humble in word and deed and truthful in jest and earnest.

O God, I have trespassed in my relationship with thee, and I have trespassed in my relationship to thy creation. O God, forgive my trespasses against thee and bear off from me my trespasses against thy creation. Enrich me with thy goodness. For thou art plenteous in forgiveness.

O God, enlighten my heart with knowledge and employ my body in thy obedience. Save me from the machinations of my heart and occupy my thoughts with thy esteem.

Prayers of the Naqshabandi Order

MAKE ME, O Lord, to give myself unto mine own penitence and to thy praises, to withdraw into penitence and blessings.

Open my mouth to bless thy holy Name: thou shalt open my lips and my mouth shall show thy praise. But for me, O Lord, sinning and not repenting, and so utterly unworthy, it were more becoming to lie prostrate before thee, and with weeping and groaning to ask pardon for my sins, than with polluted mouth to praise thee.

Howbeit, trusting in thy huge goodness, I give praise. Accept the praises I desire to sing, I an unworthy sinner, indeed unworthy. But would God I were devout and grateful unto thee.

To thee I give thanks: thee I worship, I praise, I bless, and thee I glorify.

Thou art worthy, O Lord, to receive praise and thanks, whom I, a sinner, am not worthy to call upon.

Thee I call upon, thee I worship, with the whole affection of my heart, I bless now and evermore.

LANCELOT ANDREWES: *Preces Privatae*

O LORD GOD, ever forgiving, I pray thy pardon here and hereafter, pardon in my relationships and my possessions.

Lord, hide my shortcomings and preserve my spirit within me. Take away my obstacles and keep me on the right hand and on the left, from behind and from beneath, in every undertaking.

With thee be my refuge from all that lurks below me.

ABU HAMID AL-GHAZALI: *The Reviving of Religion*

O YOU WHO believe, avoid idle supposition. Suspicion is an evil thing. Do not spy on one another and back-bite. Would any of you like to eat his brother like carrion? Loathsome thought! Hold God in awe.

Surah of the Apartments 12

BEWARE OF suspicion, the falsest of falsehoods.

Tradition noted by Ibn Hazm

A NEWSPAPER is a collection of half injustices
Which . . . spreads its curious opinion
To a million merciful and sneering men . . .
A newspaper is a court
Wherein everyone is kindly and unfairly tried
By a squalor of honest men,
A newspaper is a game
Where his error scores the player victory,
While another's skill wins death.
A newspaper is a symbol;
It is feckless life's chronicle,
A collection of loud tales
Concentrating eternal stupidities.

STEPHEN CRANE: *War is Kind*

FORGIVE, O Lord, our sanguine carelessness, our reading-up of gossip and innuendo, our reading-in of malice and ill-will, our casual appetite for easy defamation, our heedlessness of human tragedy in the daily 'press' of passing information.

Make us to read between the lines the misery and destiny of fellow men and their call to our compassion in judging and in caring. We pray so for thy truth's sake. Amen.

ISAIAH CALLETH princes thieves. What! Princes thieves? Did they stand by the highway side? Did they rob or break open any man's house or door? No! no! That is a gross kind of thieving. *Ommes diligunt munera*: 'they all love bribes'. Bribing is a princely kind of thieving.

HUGH LATIMER: Sermons

NO GRAVEN images may be
Worshipped, except the currency.

Thou shalt not steal – an empty feat,
When it's so lucrative to cheat.

Bear not false witness; let the lie
Have time on its own wings to fly.

Thou shalt not covet, but tradition
Approves all forms of competition.

ARTHUR HUGH CLOUGH: The Latest Decalogue

LORD, THY command unto the good is clear. But there is a perversity in our hearts and deviousness in our bosoms. We bring an outward service to thy law, reserving the while our own cunning and advantage. We give to the commandment the tribute of pretence and use the law itself to evade righteousness.

We circumvent thy statutes by becoming anonymous. We deplore evil and allow the big collective to pursue it. We build and blame the economic order for our alibi and hide our ungodliness in remote consent, exonerated by a customary tolerance. Evil is too abstract for our imagination, too subtle for our double-mindedness.

O God of truth, turn us to the truth, turn us to thyself. Amen.

THE ENORMOUS tragedy of the dream in the peasant's bent shoulders.

EZRA POUND: *First Pisan Canto*

WILL YOU be astonished
If these flowing fields
No longer grow crops for a privileged class,
Refuse to add to the bloodsucker's fat . . .
And that burden-hunched peasant
Stands fearless, upright as an unstringed bow,
And lifts on that back a quiverful of arrows?
Will you not be afraid?

MUFAKRUL-ISLAM: *Bengali Poems*

O LORD GOD, who has granted to men in our time an even larger empire over the material world, have mercy upon our affluence and upon our poverty, upon our pride and upon our shame.

Grant to our generation to learn the hallowing of science by the poetry of worship that we may be saved from the menace in our own competence.

Is the climax of our technology to be the dark valley of our despair? Centuries of toil have reached for the wealth we now attain.

Is it to be the easy plenty of the few amid the harsh privation of the many, a world of scientific neighbourhood across a chasm of inequality? Shall the promise of leisure be only a more wearisome curse and the long dream a proven illusion?

Let the humanity that masters nature become the servant of thy praise, whose alone and always are the power and the dominion and the glory. Amen.

I WAS AN hungred and you gave me no meat: I was thirsty and you gave me no drink: I was a stranger and you took me not in: naked, and you clothed me not: sick and in prison and you visited me not.

Then shall they answer him, saying: 'Lord, when saw we thee an hungred, or athirst, or a stranger, or naked, or sick, or in prison, and did not minister unto thee?'

Then shall he answer them saying: 'Verily I say unto you, inasmuch as you did it not to one of the least of these you did it not to me.'

The Gospel according to Matthew 25.42–5

GOD REBUKED Moses, saying: 'I am God, I fell sick; thou camest not.'

Moses said: 'O transcendent One, thou art clear of defect, what mystery is this? Explain, O Lord.'

God said unto him again: 'Wherefore didst thou not kindly ask after me when I was sick?'

He answered: 'O Lord, thou never ailest. My understanding is lost: unfold the meaning of these words.'

God said: 'Yea, a favourite and chosen slave of mine fell sick. I am he. Consider well: his infirmity is my infirmity, his sickness is my sickness.'

JALAL AL-DIN RUMI: *Mathnawi*

MAKE US, Lord,
to see and serve thy glory,
in seeing
and salving
the pain of the world.

O MY GOD, thou art my confidence: of thee I seek protection lest there be in me any source of thy unpleasing. O my God, save me from all inadequacies and let all my doings be to thy own good pleasure. O thou Lord of glory and honour, grant me the crown of knowledge, knowledge of thy unity and thy divine nature, so that I may be occupied with thee alone.

Make real to me, O God, the glory, the beauty, the excellence, the majesty, the perfection that are thine, the light and the splendour. Let me know the sweetness thereof in my own soul that I may be precluded from self-preoccupation.

Let the vision of thee keep me from the thought of myself and let me thus depart never from the keeping of thy divine laws granted by revelation.

AHMAD IBN-IDRIS: *Prayers*

LET US pray for our common good to our God, the Beneficent. May God give us grace on the left and on the right, with blessings of respect, and let his will be done.

O Lord, protect us: let our hearts be in command. Where we go give us opportunity on the right hand and on the left. Let us be obedient. Cover us.

O God, give us patience, that our lives may be dignified. Separate us from troubles that abound on earth. Give us a good compass to guide us home.

AHMAD BASHAIKH IBN HUSAIN: *Swahili Poem*

FORGIVE, O Lord, what we have been
Direct what we are,
And order what we shall be,
For thy mercy's sake. Amen.

I TAKE REFUGE with the Lord of the daybreak.

Surah of the Daybreak 1

FROM THIS fog-bound earth of ours
We take refuge in thee.
O rest of our souls,
Escaping like birds from a broken cage
To the keen, clear air, and the sunny uplands
Where thou dwellest, and with thee
Find release from meanness of spirit,
From jealousy, slander, hypocrisy,
From selfish ambition,
From the insidious darkness that broods
And breeds in our wills and hides
The vision of good and the pathway of peace.
We take refuge in thee:
Let us walk honestly in the daylight.

JOHN S. HOYLAND: *The Fourfold Sacrament*

O GOD, WITH thee I take refuge from doubt and idolatry and discord and hypocrisy and evil, from wrong seeing and from the perversion that is worship of worldly things, wealth, family and offspring.

Pilgrimage Prayers

L ORD, THOU hast created me and I am thy servant. On thy covenant and promise is my utmost reliance. With thee be my refuge from the evil I have done, pleading before thee thy mercy upon me and upon my ill-doing. Forgive me, then, for there is none that forgivest transgression, only thou, O Lord God.

ABU HAMID AL-GHAZALI: *The Reviving of Religion*

DAWN, ATTACK, booty, violence, shame, death.

By the snorting war-horses that strike fire with their hoofs as they storm forward at dawn, a single host in the midst of their dust-cloud.

Man is indeed ungrateful to his Lord; witness what he does. Violent is he in his passion for wealth. Is he not aware that their Lord is cognisant of everything about them on that day when the tombs yield up their dead and all men's hidden thoughts are public knowledge?

Surah of the War-Steeds 1–10

THE STORY, Lord, is as old as man,
Man the raider, the plunderer, the conqueror,
Defiling the light of dawn with the conspiracies
Of night,
Perverting to evil the fine instruments of nature,
Dealing fear among the tents and the homesteads
Of the unsuspecting and the weak,
Confiscating, purloining, devastating.

The passions are more subtle in our time –
The fire-power of bombs for the dust-clouds of cavalry,
Napalm and incendiary and machines in the skies,
Yet dealing the same curse of destruction,
In the same defiance of the sanctity of humankind,
The same gracelessness against the majesty on high.

By the truth of the eternal exposure,
By the reckoning of the eternal justice,
By compassion upon kin and kind,
By the awe of thy sovereignty,
Turn our deeds, O good Lord, repair our ravages,
Forgive our perversities.
O God, give peace, give grateful peace. Amen.

HOUSES GOD has permitted to be established where his Name
is commemorated and men . . . celebrate his praises.

Surah of Light 35

THE MESSAGE of these bare and empty walls
I bow to, I revere.
But don't you see? why surely you must know
That for the last time faith is with us here?
She has not crossed the threshold yet to go,
But all is swept and bare.
She has not gone for good and closed the door.
But yet the hour has struck. Kneel down and pray.
For you will pray no more.

FYODOR I. TYUTCHEV: *Russian Poems*

LORD, IN our day there are those who seek thee:
There are those who seek thee not.
Yet the *place* of worship may not well distinguish them.
Habits there evade thee, being customary,
And there are those without who seek in absence
And mark their yearning by their protest.
Make us alert who pray that the walls
Of due religion do not insulate our prayers
From the outsider's world,
Nor the outsider from our cares.
Are these homes of prayer only museums of our history?
Symbols of our culture and poems of our architects?
Is the mark of doom on every holy place?
Sceptics also have gone into museums while faith abides.
Yet prayerlessness is a heavy thing
And darkens our time most sorely.
Lord, we continue to pray: let it not be as mere
Survivors of the secular, but truly revivers of the sacred.
Amen.

O GOD, WATCH over me always, in my work, in my words, in the thoughts of my heart. O God, have mercy on me, in this world and in the world to come.

O God, have mercy on me, for I have sinned against you, mortal that I am. But kind and gentle Master, forgive me.

O God, hide not your Face from me when I come before you. Do not turn away from me when you pronounce your sentence on our lives – the lives we have lived in the open and the lives that have been ours in secret.

O God, do not let me give way to disloyalty. May the enemy find nothing in me that he can call his own. O God, sharpen my will: may it be like a sword and cut out all sinful thoughts from my heart.

O God, as you calm the sea with a word, so drive out the evil passions from my sinful nature.

SHENUTE: *Coptic Prayers of Dair al-Abyad, Egypt*

I BEG of you, my Beloved,
Pour down the dew of your mercy,
Extinguish the blackening flame,
That my faith in you may live anew.

AMIR HAMZAH: *In Darkness*

MY HELP in poverty, my refuge in distress.
My restorer in faintheartedness, my healer in distraction.
O thou who makest an end of evil deeds.
O thou in whom every complaint comes to an end.

Invocations from Hirz al-Jawshan

O GOD, THOU art God, King, manifest Truth, from of old exalted in power and might, the only abiding, the ever-living and eternal, the Almighty and supreme Disposer, the All-victorious, other than whom there is no god.

Thou art my Lord and I am thy servant. I have done evil and wronged my own soul. I have acknowledged my transgression, so pardon thou all my wrongdoings, O thou forgiving One, gracious, merciful, patient and compassionate.

O my God, I praise thee, for thou art ever praised and praise-worthy. I thank thee, who art ever thanked and worthy of thanksgiving, for all the gifts of desire thou hast granted even unto me, for the blessings of accomplishment thou hast brought to me, for all that of thy goodness thou hast bestowed upon me. By thy kindness embracing me thou hast brought me in where thy truth belongs and thou hast caused me to know it.

Thanks be to thee for all thy gracious benefits and for thy steadfast favour towards me in protecting me from calamity and answering my petitions when I call upon thee in supplication and entreaty. When I cry unto thee in sincere and humble yearning and cast myself in hope upon thee, I find thee all I need. I take refuge with thee where'er I be.

Be an ever-present neighbour to me, gracious, righteous and beneficent, watching over all things, giving victory over every adversary and forgiving all wrongdoings and transgressions and covering with a veil all unworthinesses.

AHMAD AL-TIJANI: *Prayers*

DOUBLE THEY are in their hearts, cloaking themselves to hide from him. He knows well their secret selves and what they disclose. He perceives their very hearts.

Surah of Hud 5

INASMUCH AS one couldn't condemn others without immediately judging oneself . . . one had to practise the role of a penitent to be able to end up as a judge . . . I stand before all humanity recapitulating my shame without losing sight of the effect I am producing . . . We are odd, wretched creatures and if we look back over our lives there is no lack of occasions to amaze and scandalize ourselves.

ALBERT CAMUS: *The Fall*

GOD OF truth, is there about our very penitence that which needs to be repented of?

a satisfaction in the very sense of guilt, whereby we can now condemn those we consider hardened and complacent?

a crooked recovery of our pride, in the very postures of humility, a secret arrogance in being lowly?

a fraudulent self-reproach the better to console ourselves, or to impress the world, or get a cheap immunity from action?

Make thy pardon a very fire to purge.

O THINK me worth thine anger, punish me,
Burn off my rusts and my deformity,
Restore thine image so much, by thy grace,
That thou mayest know me, and I'll turn my face.

JOHN DONNE: *Sacred Poems*

PETITION

O THOU whose mercy embraces all.
O thou whose signs are clear proof for the observant.
O thou to whom the path is open for those who
intend to find it.
O thou who in thine exaltedness art near.
O thou whose Face alone abides when all else
perishes.
O thou whose signs are in the horizon.
O thou unto whose company is all desire.
O thou who art the desire of the ascetic.
O thou in whom, obeying, the obedient find
salvation.
O thou in thanks to whom is the triumph of the
faithful.
O thou security of the fearful.
O thou whose word is always apposite.
O thou who art ever aware of what thy servants need.
O thou whose hands are stretched out in mercy.
O thou to whom all pride is hateful.
O ever wealthy, never impoverished,
O All-sufficient, never sustained.

Invocations from Hirz al-Jawshan

O THOU who art the sufficiency of those who seek of
thee to be sufficed.
O thou who seekest him that desires thee
O thou desire of him that seeks thee.

Invocations from Hirz al-Jawshan

COME FORWARD and seat yourself with ink and paper. I have matters at heart that I have longed to tell you. Now that you are near, write: 'In the Name of God.'

When you have thus acknowledged the Name of God the mighty, then let us pray for his bounty, as God shall deem fit for us. A son of Adam is nought and the world is not ours, nor is there any man that shall endure for ever . . .

This prayer of faith, if one prays, is ever granted. I am thy poor handmaiden, one burdened with many troubles: I pray thee, lighten them, O Lord, do thou unburden me. I pray to thee in haste as to matters that I cannot judge. Do thou bring me unto happiness; mayest thou deliver me from evil.

O Lord, fulfil for me the matters that I cannot accomplish, nor can I even think of one of them, that they shall come to pass.

Lord, do thou cause me to rejoice. Bring the good near to me. Remove the evil from me so that I do not meet with it.

Utendi wa Mwana Kupona, Swahili poem

O LORD GOD, make me whole, in body, in hearing and in seeing. There is no god save thou. I beseech thee, Lord, let it be well with me beyond the judgment. I ask thee life beyond the grave and the blessed vision of thy gracious Face, yearning to behold thee, all hurtful ill apart, all devious evil spent. I seek refuge with thee from wronging and from being wronged, from enmity within me and against me, and lest I come by any sin or guilt thou pardonest not.

ABU HAMID AL-GHAZALI: *The Reviving of Religion*

SHOULD ANY among you see evil activities, he should change them with his hand. If he cannot do that he should change them with his tongue. And if he cannot do that he should change them with his heart.

Tradition of the Prophet, noted by Muslim
and Ibn Khaldun

WITH OUR hands, Lord, with the touch that cares, with the skill that tends, with the healing that restores, with the energies that serve and seek the good.

This world, Lord, change it with our hands.

With our tongues, Lord,
that otherwise so lightly scorn or grossly damn it. Give us the words of sanity and peace, of compassion and goodwill, the few words that draw the sting of anger, the honest words that take the part of truth, the warm words that melt the enmity and reach the isolation of our fellows.

This world, Lord, change it through our tongues.

With our hearts, Lord,
change it with our hearts. Change it *in* our hearts and through them by our bearing of its pains, our yearning for its righteousness, our striving for its unity, our ministry to the binding of its wounds.

For always in the hearts of men its crisis turns.

Save it, Lord, in our hearts. Amen.

I sit and look out upon all the sorrows of the world, and
   upon all oppression and shame:
I see the wife misused by her husband,
I see the treacherous seducer of young women,
I mark the ranklings of jealousy and unrequited love
   attempted to be hid.
I see these sights on the earth.
I see the workings of battle, pestilence, tyranny,
I see martyrs and prisoners,
I observe the slights and degradations cast by arrogant
   persons upon labourers, the poor, and upon Negroes
   and the like:

All these – all the meanness and agony without end –
I sitting, look out upon,
See, hear and am silent.

WALT WHITMAN: *I Sit and Look Out*

LET ME rather bow, Lord, and look in,
Know my own heart, party to these wrongs,
By action or by apathy, by consent,
By guilty innocence, by connivance, by neglect,
By the very silence
When I merely sit and observe.

Kindle my heart, Lord, let me kneel and look up,
Bear in my spirit these plagues in men's deeds,
Give to the anger, the shame and the yearning,
The voice of petition,
Love men aloud in thy Presence,
Carry the vast anonymous
In the aspiration of mercy, in the arms of compassion,
Set the energy of prayer against the wiles of the devil,
Share with the travail of love in the ways of mankind,
See, hear, and cry,
Forgiveness from God. Amen.

I SAW poverty reeling in the streets,
Wracking the souls of men.
So I asked myself: What should I do?

Should I call upon the community of the poor
To thrust the sword of anger
Into the hearts of the unjust?

How pitiful it would be if we were to oppose
Evil with evil and one sin with another!

What should I do? Call upon the unjust
To lift injustice from the people?
How can a word open the hearts
That are sealed with locks of gold?

What should I do?
I possess nothing but words.
So let the wandering winds carry my words
And let me impress them on paper,
The testimony of a visionary man,
In the hope that the thirsty heart of a great man
Will find these words refreshing
And spread them among the people
And, when he comes to power,
Strike a balance between power and thought,
And join wisdom with action.

SALAH 'ABD AL-SABUR: *The Tragedy of al-Hallaj*

O GOD, OUR Father, give, we beseech thee, to all those who have the affairs of the world in their hands, a mind fitted to understand and respect rights human and divine, and lead them always to recollect that the ministration committed to them is no less than this – that they are governors of man, a creature most dear unto thee, whose praise belongs in all the earth. Amen.

HUGO GROTIUS: *De Jure Belli et Pacis*

THAT IT may please thee to bless and keep all thy people.

That it may please thee to give to all nations unity, peace and concord.

That it may please thee to give us an heart to love and fear thee and diligently to live after thy commandments.

That it may please thee to succour, help and comfort all that are in danger, necessity and tribulation.

That it may please thee to strengthen such as do stand; and to comfort and help the weak-hearted; and to raise up them that fall; and finally to beat down Satan under our feet.

That it may please thee to preserve all that travel, by land or by water or by air, all women labouring of child, all sick persons and young children and to show thy pity upon all prisoners and captives.

That it may please thee to defend and provide for the fatherless children and widows and all that are desolate and oppressed.

That it may please thee to have mercy upon all men.

That it may please thee to forgive our enemies, persecutors and slanderers and to turn their hearts.

That it may please thee to give and preserve to our use the kindly fruits of the earth, so as in due time we may enjoy them.

We beseech thee to hear us, good Lord.

THOMAS CRANMER: *The English Litany*

PEACE BE upon you and the mercy of God.
'Tis long that peace has fled from earth;
Yet the mind unexhausted quests for peace.
We've walked in crowds many: like evening birds,
Have searched for peace in shadows and in light;
We've searched for peace in the green of the fields,
In the sound of nocturnal waves and urban roads,
And in the heaven's thick shades.
'Tis long that peace
Has fled from our earth.

SHAMSUR RAHMAN: *Poems of East Bengal*

THE SWORD is a sheathed rivulet, to whose brink
Death comes to drink:
The lance a bow that drips a crimson flood
And fruits in blood.

IBN 'ABDUS: *Sword and Lance*

GOD, THOU art peace. From thee is peace and unto
thee is peace. Let us live, our Lord, in peace and
receive us in thy paradise, the abode of peace. Thine
is the majesty and the praise. We hear and we obey. Grant us
thy forgiveness, Lord and unto thee be our becoming.

Prayer at the close of Salat

AND SO I go to God to make my peace,
Where black nor white can follow to betray.
My pent-up heart to him I will release
And surely he will show the perfect way
Of life. For he will lead me and no man
Can violate or circumvent his plan.

CLAUDE MCKAY: *The Pagan Isms*

SEE, IN yonder field,
The tall cornstalks yield
Before the summer wind,
Bringing to mind
Squadrons streaming out
Of battle in sheer rout,
And the poppies red,
Where the wounded bled.

'IYAD IBN MUSA: *Corn in the Wind*

MUTUAL COUNSEL is the right pattern for them.

Surah of Counsel 38

WE BESEECH thee, O Lord our God, to set the peace of heaven within the hearts of men, that it may bind the nations also in a covenant which shall not be broken, to the honour of thy holy Name.

Cleanse us with the cleanness of thy truth and guide our steps in inward holiness.

Give concord and peace to us and to all living on the earth, as thou gavest to our fathers, when they prayed to thee, believing truly and ready to obey the All-powerful, the All-holy.

Grant to those who rule and lead us on earth to use aright the sovereignty thou hast bestowed upon them. Lord, make their counsels conform to what is good and pleasing unto thee, that, using with reverence and peace and gentleness the power thou hast granted them, they may find favour in thy sight. Thou only hast the means to do this, this and more than this. Glory be thine, now in the present age and age after age.

CLEMENT OF ROME: *Epistle to the Corinthians*

LET THE peace of God rule in your hearts, to which also you are called in one body; and be thankful.

Epistle to the Colossians 3.15

SONG OF kinsmen as they water their camels:

They are all here ready,
They belong to us.
How splendid and useful they are!
And they are standing ready.

I set my foot on the well,
O Master of the world,
O God, the Just, make our task easy.

You will be cooled,
Come forward slowly.
Put your mouth to it with blessing.
It is devoid of evil:
Your shrivelled bones
Are now moist and full again.

When they are standing ready,
And the clansmen all are present,
None must leave till all are watered.

Camel-Watering Chant, Somaliland

LORD OF the world, grant us wonder, give us reverence, subdue us to courtesy, guide us to unity, school us to gratitude.
Let us know our mastery to be of thy mercy. Let thy peace rule, in the great and in the small.

Give us peace with thee,
Peace with men, peace with ourselves,
And free us from all fear.

DAG HAMMARSKJÖLD: *Markings*

AND WAR is not aught but what you know well
And have tasted oft.
When ye set her on foot,
Ye start with words of little praise,
But the mind of her grows with her growth,
Till she burst into blazing flame.

ZUHAIR: Mu'allaqah of the Jahiliyyah

FORGIVENESS HAD we for Hind's sons:
  We said: 'These men our brothers are:
The days may bring them yet again
  They be the folk that once they were.'

But when the ill stood clear and plain
  And naked wrong was bare to day
And nought was left but bitter hate,
  We paid them in the coin they gave.

We strode, as stalks the lion forth
  At dawn, a lion wrathful eyed:
Blows rained we, dealing shame on shame,
  And humbling pomp and quelling pride . . .

The Banu Zimman, poem of the Jahiliyyah

LORD, MAKE me an instrument of thy peace. Where
there is hatred, let me bring love: where there is
injury, pardon: where there is doubt, faith: where
there is despair, hope: where there is darkness, light: where
there is sadness, joy: and all for thy mercy's sake.

FRANCIS OF ASSISI

THE MORE he strives to injure me
  The greater is my clemency.
So when the wick is cut, its light
  Shines all the clearer through the night.

IBN AL-HAJJ: Poem

YOU ARE straitened in your own selves: . . . be enlarged.

Second Epistle to the Corinthians 6.12–13

OUT OF Ireland have we come.
Great hatred, little room,
Maimed us at the start.
I carry from my mother's womb
A fanatic heart.

W. B. YEATS: *Collected Poems*

LORD, THERE are many such,
Dwelling in narrow resentments,
Embittered by wrongs that others have inflicted,
Confined to harsh enmities,
Imprisoned in spirit by despair at evil deeds,
Drained of hope and bereft of peace,
Left to great hatred in this world.
Have mercy, good Lord, upon all these
Whose world, through human malice,
Despairs of human kindness.
Judge and turn their oppressors.
Release again, for the fearful,
The springs of trust and goodness.
Give them liberty of heart
The liberty of those who leave room
For the judgment of God.
Enlarge our hearts, O God,
That we may do battle against evil
And bear the sorrows of the weary,
And seek and serve thy will.
Great art thou, O Lord.
There is nought that is a match for thee. Amen.

O my Lord, enlarge my heart.

Surah of Ta Ha 26

Petition ⟿ 73

WHEN MY servants ask of me, indeed, I am near . . .
When comes God's help? Surely, God's help is near.

Surah of the Cow 186, 214

PRISONERS EVERYWHERE.
Send me all you have
Fears screams and boredom
Fishermen of all beaches
Send me all you have
Empty nets and seasickness . . .
To my address . . . any cafe
Any street in the world
I'm preparing a huge file
About human suffering
To present to God
Once it's signed by the lips of the hungry
And the eyelids of those still waiting.
You wretched everywhere
What I fear most is
God could be illiterate.

MUHAMMAD AL-MAGHUT: *The Poet-Postman*

KIRIYALAYSON, LORD, O Lord, your world is a tragedy on
which the curtain rose when time began.

I shed the tears of others for their sake. Hear, O Lord.

LOUIS 'AWAD: *Pyramid Poem*

IF, LORD, we have the tears of others sometimes in our
eyes, seeing in a caring proxy the reasons why they
grieve: do we not call upon your mercy as wider, surer,
more resourceful than our own? Your unfailing grace – on
which we plead – has been our school against indifference, O
Lord of utmost mercy. Amen.

YOUR SOUL may well be consumed in pain for yearning after the unbelieving.

Surah of the Cave 6

CAN BREAD give strength, or feed,
Unless it first be broken for the need?
Or shall the vine, with grapes uncrushed,
For others yield its wine?

JALAL AL-DIN RUMI: *Mathnawi*

O LORD, WHOSE service requires all that a man has, grant us in our hearts the grace of self-giving and the power of sacrifice.

Fit us for the costs of truth and the labours of compassion. Make us able for the calling which is not by power or might but only by thy Spirit.

Enable us to live in courage beyond the appearance of the present or the entail of the past. Teach us the strength by which to hold with any lost cause of thine until it can be truly won.

Grant us the benediction of the peacemakers in the things of reconciliation that force and state cannot attain. Give us endurance, not grim and hard, but gentle and joyous in the peace of thy eternity. Show us the long-suffering that is more strong than anger, more ultimate than hate.

As by broken bread the peoples of the world are fed, so make us to serve their good by a ready consecration of our wills, according to thy purpose, who art blessed in mercy, now and evermore. Amen.

I F IT is said to them: 'Worship the compassionate Lord,' they say: 'What is this – the compassionate Lord? Are we to worship just at your behest?' And they are only the more alienated.

Surah of Salvation 60

I HAVE NO other pictures of the world apart from those which express evanescence and callousness, vanity and anger, emptiness, or hideous, useless hate . . . futile and sordid fits of rage, cries suddenly blanketed by silence, shadows swallowed up for ever by the night. What else have I to say?

EUGENE IONESCO: *Notes*

G RANT TO us, O merciful Lord, whom thou hast called to faith in thy compassion:

a mind for the distrust that besets our fellow men at the very sound of such assurance, hurt and broken as they are by the stresses of the world and the oppressiveness of evil;

a heart to serve them in the goodness of truth, a heart large enough to take the honesty of their scepticism and meet it in the honesty of faith;

a patience in the commendation of truth resourceful enough, by the gift of thy mercy, to outstay the suspicions of the cynical, the alienations of the angry, the fears of the betrayed, the apathy of the defeated;

a gentleness fashioned after the pattern of thy mercy, O compassionate Lord of men. Amen.

DID HE not find thee an orphan and sheltered thee?
Find thee wandering and led thee?
Find thee needy and sufficed thee?

Then do not oppress the orphan,
Nor repel the suppliant.
The grace of your Lord – let that be your theme.

Surah of the Forenoon 6–11

WOULD THAT you knew what the steep is!
It is the freeing of the slave,
Or giving food in the hungry day
To an orphan near of kin,
Or to some needy soul in his distress.
Such are believers indeed:
Patience and mercy are their counsel,
Their counsel to each other.

Surah of the Land 11–17

IN PART we know it, Lord,
The hard road of compassion,
The strenuous demands of mercy,
The steep ascent of heaven.
But the counsels of bitterness and hatred
Come so quickly to our lips,
So plausibly to our reason.
We do well to be angry, contemptuous, outraged,
We, the exploited, the displaced, the cheated,
We, the ill-used.
Yet make our distresses patient, our counsels gentle.
Let us not refuse the rugged climb
Into lovingkindness,
Out of mere level orthodoxy
And a faith of the shadows.
Make us believers indeed, after thy heart. Amen.

ASPIRATIONS HALF-MAST, hopes benumbed,
Desires under pessimism succumbed . . .
Some humiliation always to stab the rejoicing,
Every smile moist with a touch of chagrin.
Faces and features corrupted by artifice,
Laughter poisoned with innate malice . . .
Only the outer clothing, the gorgeous attire,
Hearts weeping for bitterness of life's satire . . .
Neither passion, nor excitement, freshness nor gaiety.
This is all our entire society.

JOSH MALIHABADI: *Our Society*

THE NIGHT, the street, street-lamp, drugstore,
A meaningless dull light about.
You may live twenty-five years more
All will still be there. No way out.

You die. And all again
Will be repeated as before.
The cold rippling of a canal.
The night, the street, street-lamp, drugstore.

ALEXANDER A. BLOK: *Russian Poems*

OUR CRY . . .
    the things we feel but cannot pray . . .
Let our cry *come* . . .
    from our despair it comes, from our fear . . .

Let our cry come, *Lord* . . .
    Name we cannot comprehend, power we cannot tell,
    Love we cannot trace . . .

Let our cry come, Lord, *unto thee.*

S AY: I take refuge with the Lord of the daybreak.

Surah of Daybreak 2

H E IS the Lord of the points of the sunrise and Lord of the setting suns. Which of the blessings of the Lord will you discount and deny?

Surah of Al-Rahman 17–18

Lo, IN the sanctuaried East,
Day, a dedicated priest
In all his robes pontifical exprest,
Lifteth slowly, lifteth sweetly,
From its orient tabernacle drawn,
Yon orbed sacrament confest
Which sprinkles benediction through the dawn:
And when the grave procession's ceased,
The earth with due illustrious rite
Blessed . . .
Sets, for high close of the mysterious feast . . .
Within the flaming monstrance of the West . . .

FRANCIS THOMPSON: *Orient Ode*

L ORD OF East and West, the steady unfailing light of our common day, renewing and resting the face of the earth in the cycle of a sure fidelity and gentle grace, kindle daily our perception of the benison of being, that the sun go not down on our wrath or sloth.

Shame by the light of day the passions and enmities of the dark, the conspiracies of self-interest, the habits of suspicion, the distortions of power in the intercourse of nations and the conduct of our private selves.

Teach us to walk as children of the day that the wealth of nations may be seen and served aright, in awe of your great Name, O Lord of eve and morn. Amen.

OUR HEARTS have built this sanctuary to the glory of your Name before ever hand laid stone upon another. May the temples we build within ourselves be as beautiful as the house built of stone. May your kindliness bring you to dwell in both kinds of temple. For our hearts, no less than these stones, bear the mark of your Name.

God, who is All-powerful, could have made himself a house as easily as he brought the world into existence, with a wave of his hand. But he preferred to build man himself instead and man in turn to build for him. Blessed be the mercy that showed us such love.

He is Infinite and we are finite: he built us the world and we build him a house. What a wonderful thing that men can build a house for the God of all power, who is present everywhere, whom nothing escapes. He lives among us out of his compassion towards us and he binds us to himself with his love.

To him be all praise and glory and dominion.

BALAI OF ALEPPO: *Syriac hymn for a church hallowing*

TO PURIFY oneself, to remember the Name of the Lord and to pray – this is well-being.

Surah of the Most High 14–15

WE PRAY Almighty God that he will set us among those whom he has guided and led to the truth, those whom he has inspired to think on him so that they forget him not, those whom he has preserved from the evil of the flesh so that they choose him above all else, those whom he has devoted to himself so that they worship none save him.

ABU HAMID AL-GHAZALI: *The Deliverer from Wandering*

AN OLIVE neither of the east nor of the west, whose oil is almost incandescent without the touch of fire: light upon light . . .

Surah of Light 34

THOUGH IT is out of the east that the sun rises . . .
It burns and blazes with inward fire
Only when it escapes the shackles of east and west . . .
That it may subject all horizons to its mastery.

MUHAMMAD IQBAL: *Javid Nama*

I CALL UPON thee, O God, by the Names inscribed around thy throne. I call upon thee by the Names written upon thy Seat. I call upon thee, O God, by the Name written upon the leaves of the olive tree.

I call upon thee, O God, in the mighty Names with which thou hast named thyself, those of them that I have known and those I have not known.

Prayers of the Naqshabandi Order

O LORD GOD, who hast made us of different nations but one mankind, whose light rises in the east and reaches unto the west yet belongs to the entire heaven and to all the earth, grant us in thy light to see light.

So govern and order our human diversities that they may serve the whole peace of men, that from the rising of the sun to its going down, thy Name may be great among the nations and the nations blessed in the confession of thy Name, who art exalted above all thy works. Amen.

S AY: 'CALL upon God or call upon the Merciful: make either invocation, for his are the most excellent Names. Be neither strident nor speechless. Set your heart on the due path of prayer.'

Surah of the Night Journey 110

OUR CONFIDENCE is in thee,
Who art from the beginning of the creation.
Thou hast opened our eyes within us
That we might know thee, who alone art Most High.

Curb the loftiness of the proud,
Frustrate the designs of the evil-seekers,
Lift up the lowly and bring the mighty down.
Give riches and poverty, life and death.

Thou art the God of all flesh.
Into the deeps thou dost gaze,
Vigilant over all that men are doing.
Thou art our help in danger
And savest us from despair
Creator and sustainer of all that is spiritual.

We pray thee, Lord, to help and defend us,
Deliver the oppressed, pity the insignificant,
Raise the fallen, show thyself to the needy,
Heal the sick and bring back the wanderers,
Feed the hungry, lift up the weak,
Take off the prisoners' chains,
Let every nation come to know thou art God.

The earth is thy creation, Lord,
Such competence is thine in creating,
Such goodness is apparent in the world we behold.
Forgive us our sins, our injustice, our warring deeds.

CLEMENT OF ROME: *Epistle to the Corinthians*

O LORD, save thy people and bless thine heritage:
Govern them and lift them up for ever.
Day by day we magnify thee,
And we worship thy Name ever, world without end.
Vouchsafe, O Lord, to keep us this day without sin,
O Lord, have mercy upon us, have mercy upon us:
O Lord, let thy mercy lighten upon us,
As our trust is in thee.
O Lord, in thee have I trusted,
Let me never be confounded.

Te Deum Laudamus

TRULY IN God have I trusted, my Lord and your Lord.

Surah of Hud 56

O GOD, I could not do without thy help and thy right-eousness, thy goodness, thy strength and thy beneficence, not even for the twinkling of an eye.

I am thy servant, O God, from the time thou didst set me in this vale of soul-making, of thought and experience, that thou mightest observe what I sent forward into the world of immortality and decision, the abode of the blest.

Make me, O God, thy free man.

O God, I have no thought of thee but what is beautiful. I see in thee nought but graciousness. Thy goodness is to me all-embracing. Thy works in my sight are perfect. Ever sure is thy mercy and thy righteousness is full of forgiveness. Thy bountifulness toward me is constant and perpetual and unremitting are thy benefits.

AHMAD AL-TIJANI: *Prayers*

DEATH LEANS to death! nor shall your vigilance
Prevent him from whate'er he would possess.

Dark leans to dark! the passions of a man
Are turned about all transitory things.

The centuries are morsels of the night.

ABU-L-'ALA AL-MA'ARI: *Quatrains*

THUS COMMAND my heart and soul:
    'Let us forward go.'
Thought under iron-heels,
Ideals under house-arrest,
Fill my cup of woe,
    'Let us forward go.'

'ABDUL-HALIM JOSH: *Sindhi Poems*

O LORD GOD, who hast called thy worshippers to stead-fastness in perplexity and to a good courage in the face of evil, renew in us in this our day the strength of will and patience of soul whereby thy servants before us fulfilled their calling in thy will.

Let no discouragement deflect us from the straight path and no dismay deter us from our avowed intent to follow it. Give us boldness that we may defy all that – thy grace apart – would daunt our spirits and beset our way with fears.

Give us a sure confidence in the issue of our lives that no powers of earth or hell may hold us in the thrall of false anxiety. Rather let us labour night and day to make good a pilgrim's constancy, come wind, come weather. By thine aid and goodness, hear our prayer.

Adapted from JOHN BUNYAN: *The Pilgrim Song*

I SAY UNTO you: 'Love your enemies, bless them that curse you, do good to them that hate you, and pray for them which despitefully use you, and persecute you, that you may be the children of your Father who is in heaven. For he makes his sun rise on the evil and on the good and he sends rain on the just and on the unjust.'

The Gospel according to Matthew 5.44–5

BROADCAST WIDELY if you can
The benevolence you plan,
Troubling not if near or far
Its receiving stations are.

So the rain has little care
What it fall upon, or where,
Irrigating equally
Barren rock and fertile lea.

SIRAJ OF ANDALUSIA: *Poems*

I ASK OF God mercy and forgiveness and I pray that he would be pleased to lead us to the fountain of the pure knowledge of himself. For he is gracious and liberal in his kindness.

Peace be to you my brother, whom it is my duty to aid, and the mercy and blessing of God be upon you.

IBN TUFAYL: Concluding prayer in *Alive, Son of Alert*

MY BROTHERS, the love of God is a hard love. It demands total self-surrender.

ALBERT CAMUS: *The Plague*

HAD THE truth followed their passions, the heavens and the earth and all within them would have altogether gone awry. But we have brought men their Reminder, flout it as they do.

Surah of the Believers 73

OBSERVE THE conduct of these people closely:
Find it estranging, if not very strange;
Hard to explain even if it is the custom,
Hard to explain even if it is the rule.
Observe the smallest action, seeming simple,
With distrust. Enquire if a thing be necessary
Especially if it is common.
We particularly ask you,
When a thing continually occurs,
Not, on that account, to find it natural
In an age of bloody confusion,
Ordered disorder, planned caprice,
And dehumanized humanity, lest all things
Be held unalterable.

BERTOLT BRECHT: *Plays*

LORD, SAVE us from easy acquiescence in the way of things. Let us not think the deceits around our senses the only mirror of humanity. Keep our minds that they move in more than headlines and detect the shape of prejudice or the slant of greed. Alert us against the cheap purveyors.

Make us open to the judgment that saves because it faithfully condemns. Let us not resign to sub-humanities. Give us humour and ardour to deplore and not disdain, to repudiate and yet transform. Our very restlessness denies us a deceptive rest and the eternal Reminder abides, the more patient if the more refused, and to thee is our returning. Amen.

A MAN said to the universe:
'Sir! I exist.'
'However', replied the universe,
'That fact has not created in me
A sense of obligation'.

STEPHEN CRANE: *War is Kind*

WE WILL show them our signs in the horizons and in themselves, that it may yet be evident to them that it is the truth. Does it not suffice thee that thy Lord is witness over all things? Does he not encompass everything that they should be thus in doubt that it is with him they have to do?

Surah of the Expounded Signs 53–4

DOUBTERS, LORD, are many in our day
People daunted by the fear of their irrelevance,
Oppressed by the vast infinity of space,
Redundant in the very progress of technology,
Powerless within the organization of power,
Finding no meaning to their insignificance.

Make us, Lord, to serve their reassurance wisely,
Lest the sense of thy mercy
Seem an empty wistfulness
They will not stay to test,
Suspecting we are shallow men
Or merely doctrinaire.

So dwell in our thoughts and make godly our ways
That men may read thy signs within them
And without and it may suffice them
To know that thou art God, God alone,
Embracing all things, and knowing
Even where thou art not known. Amen.

WE HAVE sent down iron with its mighty potential and its diverse utility to men, that God may know those who are for him and his messengers, siding with the hidden mystery.

Surah of Iron 25

LOOK! HERE I stand, among lathes, hammers,
Furnaces and forges, among a hundred comrades.
    There are iron-forged spaces above me,
    Girders and angle bars on the sides,
    Rising seventy feet, bending right and left.
They are tied to the cupola rafters and
Like a giant's shoulders support the whole iron frame.
    They are impetuous, sweeping, strong.
    They require a still greater strength.
I look at them and I stand straighter;
New iron blood pours into my veins,
And I am growing taller, steel shoulders
And immeasurably strong arms grow out from me.
I merge with the building's iron.
Then I stretch myself,
With my shoulders I push out the rafters
    The highest girders and roof . . .
    And I am going to shout one single iron phrase:
The victory will be ours!

ALEKSEI K. GASTEV: *Russian Poems*

BY THY leave, O Lord, from ore and mine, in furnace and foundry, with lathe and bore, we shape our tools and take our powers. Civilization through metallurgy, culture by electronics, iron and the soul. Grant us, we pray thee, so to wield power as to learn reverence, so to take the force that we may bow to the mystery of nature, so to yield to thy authority that we rightly know our own. Amen.

THAT THOU mayest rightly obey power, her bounds know. Those past, her nature and her name is changed. To be then humble to her is idolatry.

JOHN DONNE: *Third Satire*

MAN INDEED transgresses in thinking himself his own master. For to your Lord shall all things return . . . Nay! Do not obey him: worship and draw closer [to God].

Surah of the Blood Clot 6, 7, 8–19

TRULY IDOLATRY is great wrong.

Surah of Luqman 12

LORD, AROUND us are the manifold works of men: states, structures of trade and power, machines and media, principalities of science and race, customs and cultures – all by the dominion entrusted to men's hands under your sovereignty.

With these vast achievements come also usurpations and injustices, tyrannies and prides, working the alienation of the very humanity that boasts them.

Save us, Lord, from every false worship, from all deceiving arrogance. Let us be absolute for thee alone. Keep us from every idolatry of thing, or power, or thought, or means, or claim.

For yours is the Kingdom of the heavens and of the earth and in your rule is our peace. Amen.

D O NOT live on usury doubling your wealth many times over: have fear of God.

Surah of the House of 'Imran 129

T HOSE WHO devour usury shall be as men deranged by the touch of Satan when they stand before God.

Surah of the Cow 275

WITH *USURA* hath no man a house of good stone
each block cut smooth and well fitting
that design might cover their face . . .
with *usura* . . .
no picture is made to endure nor to live with
but it is made to sell and sell quickly . . .
Usura rusteth the chisel.
It rusteth the craft and the craftsman,
It gnaweth the thread in the loom.
None learneth to weave gold in her pattern . . .
Usura slayeth the child in the womb . . .
Corpses are set to banquet
at behest of *usura*.

EZRA POUND: *Canto XLV*

FROM THE blight of graceless consumption,
From the deceit of advertisement,
From death in plenty,
From the tyranny of acquisition,
From the bondage of the cash-nexus,
From the compounded evils of crude interest,
From the exploitation of our fellows,
From the coarseness of riches,
From the banality of wasting possession,
From empty satedness with technology,
From the the curse of *usura*.
God save this people: good Lord, deliver us. Amen.

THEY ONLY betray themselves and realize it not. For in their hearts there is a sickness.

Surah of the Cow 9–10

MANKIND IS sick, the world distempered lies . . .
The wise and good like kind physicians are,
That strive to heal them by their care.
For since the sickness is (they find)
A sad distemper of the mind:
All railings they impute,
All injuries, unto the sore disease
They are expressly come to ease.
If we would to the world's distempered mind
Impute the rage which there we find,
We might . . . pity all the griefs we see,
Anointing every malady with precious oil and balm;
And while ourselves are calm,
Our art improve to rescue them . . .
But let's not fondly our own selves beguile:
If we revile 'cause they revile,
Ourselves infected with their sore disease . . .

THOMAS TRAHERNE: *Poems*

GIVE THY saving health, O Lord, to all nations.
In the cruse of hatred there is no oil and wine
To heal the wounds of men:
No sanity in the distempers of anger and contention,
No ease for sorrows from hearts that only curse,
From wills that take the contagion they denounce,
From minds that sicken, being sickened.
Heal us, Lord, within, that we may be thy healers
In the world around. Let us bear away the malice
In the steadfast health of love, in the whole life
Of thy compassion. Amen.

Go, my songs, to the lonely and the unsatisfied . . .
Speak against unconscious oppression,
Speak against the tyranny of the unimaginative . . .
Go to the hideously wedded,
Go to them whose failure is concealed . . .
Go in a friendly manner,
Go with an open speech,
Be eager to find new evils and new good.
Be against all forms of oppression.
Go to those who are thickened with middle age,
To those who have lost their interest . . .
Go out and defy opinion.

EZRA POUND: *Commission*

COME, my soul, come in petition,
Come with all these in the caring of your spirit.
Speak with the lips of the imaginative:
Bear the unloved, the unloving,
To the compassion of God. Remember
The thwarted, the cheated, the cheating,
The dropouts, the angry, the broken.
Set the 'So be it' of the will of God
Against 'Thus it is' of men's ill-doing, ill-shaping.

Come with open speech,
Come in the friendship of hope.
Strengthen the subtle cords
That bind the passion of peace
With the woes of the world.
In the travail of righteousness come,
Bring the lonely, the empty, the sated,
To the authority of God.

So teach us to pray. Amen.

A

RE THERE locks upon your hearts?

Surah of Muhammad 27

'TIS LOVE alone can hearts unlock . . .
What magic bolts, what mystic bars . . .
Maintain the will!
Disband dull fears, give faith the day.
It is love's siege and sure to be
Your triumph through his victory.
'Tis cowardice that keeps this field
And want of courage not to yield.
Yield, then, O yield, that love may win
The fort at last and let life in . . .
This fort of your fair self, if't be not won,
He is repulsed indeed, but you're undone.

RICHARD CRASHAW: *Poems*

SAVE US, O Lord, from hardness, from barredness,
Of heart.

Let thy coming, Lord, find our compassion open,
Open to the lonely, the demanding, the uninteresting,
Open to receive, to welcome, to befriend.

Let thy coming, Lord, find our conscience open.
Open to the reproach of thy holy law,
Open to the rebuke of righteousness,
Open to ask forgiveness, open to find mercy.

Let thy coming, Lord, find our wonder open,
Open to thy signs, alerted to mystery,
Kindling to gratitude,
Open to greet with joy the benedictions of the earth.

The key thou gavest me to turn, I yield to thee. Amen.

WE BESEECH thee, Lord,
Remember all for good:
Have pity upon all, O sovereign Lord.

Fill our garners with all manner of store,
Preserve our marriages in peace and concord,
  Nourish our infants,
  Lead forward our youth,
  Sustain our aged,

Comfort the faint-hearted,
  Gather together the dispersed,
  Restore the wanderers,
  Set free the troubled with unclean spirits,
Travel with the travellers,
  Stand forth for the widow, shield the orphan,
  Rescue the captive and heal the sick.

Remember, O God, all who need thy great compassion,
And upon all pour out thy rich pity.

For thou, Lord, art the succour of the succourless,
  The hope of the hopeless,
  The Saviour of the tempest-tossed,
  The harbour of the voyager,
The physician of the sick.

For thou knowest every man and his petition,
Every house and its need,
Being the God of all spirits and of all flesh.

LANCELOT ANDREWES: *Preces Privatae*

A VISITOR FROM Cordoba informed me, when I asked him for news of that city, that he had seen our dwelling, that its traces were well-nigh obliterated and its way-marks effaced . . . I remembered the days I had passed in that fair mansion . . . now scattered by the hand of exile and torn to pieces by the finger of expatriation. I saw in my mind's eye the ruin of that noble house in whose midst I had grown to man's estate.

IBN HAZM: *The Ring of the Dove*

L ORD OF mercy and God of the human family, you have conjoined our being and our dwelling in token of your compassion. We thank you for the love of land and landscape in our hearts, for the birthmark of home by which we know ourselves.

Remember all whose lives are broken in our time by dispossession, by homelessness and exile, who live in tented privation while others occupy their soil and farm their lands.

Arm us against the casual forgetfulness of what for others is the unforgettable, the shadowed future, the shattered past.

In your ancient law, you commanded a care for the stranger within our gates. What of our gates that make the stranger strangers within their own gates, embittered and undone?

Sustain with your mercy the agencies of ministry to refugees, the measures for present relief and future reconcil-iation. Subdue the community of nations in their passions and their policies to your righteous will that justice may come again and peace lift up her lovely face. Amen.

SEEK YE first the Kingdom of God, and his righteousness.

The Gospel according to Matthew 6.33

O GOD, THOU hast been gracious unto us and hast bestowed conscience upon us. It is a spirit from thee. What it enjoins and what it prohibits are alike thine. Whosoever obeys it obeys thee: the one who flouts it flouts thee. Thou hast left to us the obeying of it.

Keep our doings within the bounds of conscience. O God, do not let us be so encumbered with the things of this world that we transgress the bounds of conscience. O God, so inspire us that we follow no other guidance. Teach us not to override it for any alternative however impressive and to set up no idols to be worshipped or esteemed as good.

For outside conscience there is no good. O God, guide those who preside over human affairs that they establish no order that will oblige others to transgress conscience and that they do not inflict on others wrongs that are immediate and concrete for the sake of something supposedly and ultimately good for society. For this is the origin of our tragic trouble and the source of the evil within us.

O God, thou hast endowed conscience with no material force to compel our reluctant obedience. So give us inwardly a spiritual compulsion in which we will follow it out of choice and delight . . . O God, guide thy servants who have gone almost irretrievably astray. Thou art the hearer and the answerer.

KAMEL HUSSEIN: *City of Wrong*

WHO BUYS my thoughts
Buys not a cup of honey
That sweetens every taste.
He buys the throb of young Afric's soul,
The soul of teeming millions,
Hungry, naked, sick,
Yearning, pleading, waiting.

Who buys my thoughts
Buys not some false pretence
Of oracles and tin gods.
He buys the thoughts projected by the mass
Of restless youths, who are born
Into deep and clashing cultures,
Sorting, questioning, watching.

Who buys my thoughts
Buys the spirit of the age
The unquenching fire that smoulders
And smoulders
In every living heart
That is true and noble and suffering:
It burns o'er all the earth,
Destroying, chastening, cleansing.

DENNIS OSADEBAY: *Poems*

LORD, HEAR the prayers of our thoughts,
    Direct the thoughts of our prayers.
        Make plain thy will,
        Make sure our obedience.
In thy mercy,
    Hallow, rule, teach, and renew our aspirations,
    And bend our hearts to their achieving. Amen.

COME LET us now enquire
How each is faring. Let us gain –
If gain we may, upon this plain
Of trouble vast where pastures pure,
From fear secure, are not to find –
The spirit's far desire.

SHAMS AL-DIN HAFIZ: *Wild Deer*

DO NOT despair of the Spirit of God. It is only those who give the lie to him who despair of the Spirit of God.

Surah of Joseph 87

I PRAY THEE, Lord, let my way be resolute and my purpose firm in thy good counsel. Grant me, O Lord, the boon of gratefulness for thy grace, the beauty that belongs with thy worship. Give me a pure and reverent heart, uprightness of character, a tongue that speaks right and deeds that are worthy, O Lord God.

ABU HAMID AL-GHAZALI: *The Reviving of Religion*

ETERNAL GOD,
    the light of the minds that know thee,
    the joy of the hearts that love thee,
    the strength of the wills that serve thee,
Grant us
    so to know thee that we may truly love thee,
    so to love thee that we may freely serve thee,
whom to serve is perfect freedom,
    to the glory of thy holy Name.

The Gelasian Sacramentary

O MY PEOPLE, how is it with me that I call you to salvation and you call me to the fire?

Surah of the Believers 41

LET US lie in wait for the righteous man, because he is not for our turn, and he is clean contrary to our doings: he upbraideth us with offending the law . . . The very sight of him is a burden to us, because his manner of life is unlike that of others and his ways are strange. We are esteemed of him as false coin and he abstaineth from our ways as from filthiness . . . Let us test him with insults and torture, that we may find out how gentle he is and make trial of his forbearance . . . But they knew not the mysteries of God.

The Wisdom of Solomon 2.12–22

WE THANK thee, O God, for the patience of truth in thy servants the prophets, of whom evil men made trial in perversity and contempt. In their integrity for thy Name, thy law and thy mercy keep righteous faith with the world. Even in the sign of hatred men recognize their prophets. By the evil that they bear wrong stands at once condemned and overcome. In their steadfastness, thy power fulfils its righteous purpose.

For their goodly fellowship, we praise thee, O God. Lord of thy faithful servants, make us to learn both our judgment and our salvation, that in our time we may be doers of thy will and servants of thy glory, to the praise of thy Name. Amen.

LISTEN

To the deep pulse of Africa beating in the mist of
    forgotten villages.
See the tired moon comes down to her bed on the slack
    sea,
The laughter grows weary, the story tellers even
Are nodding their heads like a child on the back of its
    mother.
The feet of the dancers grow heavy and heavy the voice
    of the answering choirs.
It is the hour of night, the night that dreams,
Leaning upon this hill of clouds, wrapped in its long,
    milky cloth.
The roofs of the huts gleam tenderly. What do they say
    so secretly to the stars?
Inside, the fire goes out among intimate smells, that are
    acrid and sweet.

LÉOPOLD SÉDAR SENGHOR: *Night in Senegal*

O BLESS this people, Lord, who seek their own face
under the mask and can hardly recognize it . . .
O bless this people that breaks its bond . . .
And with them, all the peoples of Europe,
All the peoples of Asia,
All the peoples of Africa,
All the peoples of America,
Who sweat blood and sufferings.
And see, in the midst of these millions of waves
The sea swell of the heads of my people.
And grant to their warm hands that they may clasp
The earth in a girdle of brotherly hands,
Beneath the rainbow of thy peace.

LÉOPOLD SÉDAR SENGHOR: *Prayer for Peace*

A CTIVE IS he, day in and day out.

Surah of Al-Rahman 29

HIS LEAST act every day is that he despatches three
   armies:
One from the loins of the fathers to the mothers,
In order that the seed may grow in the womb:
One army from the wombs to the earth,
That the world may be filled with male and female:
One army from the earth to what lies beyond death . . .

JALAL AL-DIN RUMI: *Mathnawi*

NOT A day passes, not a minute or second
   without an accouchement:
Not a day passes, not a minute or second
   without a corpse . . .
. . . and the living looking upon it.

WALT WHITMAN: *To Think of Time*

LORD, IN thee we live and have our being.
Thou art he who brings to birth and brings to death.
Thou dost not weary of mankind,
But givest day by day the gift of life,
Making men and women the creators
In the tireless procession of the generations,
Fearfully and wonderfully made.
Grant us in our time the hallowing of the womb
And reverence for the mystery of life.
Teach us, in the teeming world, the due trust of birth,
To keep faith with the newly born, the yet unborn,
Lest the crowded earth shall not suffice them.
And in the midst of life, we pray for those in death,
In the ceaseless exodus of the departing.
Thine it is to summon, thine to have mercy and to save. Amen.

O LORD, GRANT us in our wives and in our offspring the joy of our eyes.

Surah of Salvation 74

GOD THAT mad'st her well regard her,
How she is so fair and bonny . . .
From here to there to the sea's border
Dame nor damsel there's not any
Hath of perfect charms so many.
Thoughts of her are of dream's order.
God that mad'st her well regard her.

EZRA POUND: *Dieu! Qui L'a faicte*

WE ARE delighted with the new arrival. God give him a large share of his name and the utmost of that after which he is called . . . It is fortunate for one who arrives into this world with the spring smiling on his face, bidding him welcome with its roses and its flowers, presenting him with its rich verdure . . . I ought not indeed to congratulate . . . but joy overcame me and made me indiscreet.

ABU-L-'ALA AL-MA'ARI: *Letters*

LORD, GRANT us joy of our wives and children. Make reverence the garment of our love and hallowing the benediction of our homes. By the surety of the troth we keep make safe the troths of all. For the joy of our eyes grant us faith in our souls. Make us and ours ready for all seasons, gay and grave. Make our loves true and in their truth make our nation glad.

Lord, hear our prayer: our prayer, Lord, hear. Amen.

GOD KNOWS that my wood produces no fire. . . [yet] there is no question that our hearts meet in affection, and that our spirits shake hands every day, nay, every hour.

The bonds of our loves, Lord, hallow and enrich.

I have been awaiting intelligence of you as the traveller who has lagged behind the caravan asks where his comrades are gone, or the pasture-hunter enquires where the rain has fallen.

The cares of our loves, Lord, hallow and direct.

I can only hope that the shell of your fortune may produce a pearl of rare price and that the buds of your times may open into the sweetest flower.

The hopes of our loves, Lord, hallow and fulfil.

I beg you will not drive your reed over an answer to this letter, for I know so well what is in your mind that I need not give trouble to your hand. God who is Almighty will protect you . . . and may the rising sun each morning bring you recruited strength.

The pledges of our loves, Lord, hallow and renew.

I shall preserve my affection for you as the rhyming syllable is preserved from alteration of vowel or consonant . . . For our love is in a well-guarded place, secure against time's ravages.

The love of our loves, Lord, keep in thy truth.

ABU-L-'ALA AL-MA'ARI: Greetings in his *Letters*

WHEN THE [female] infant, buried alive, shall ask: For what sin was she slain?

Surah of the Darkened Sun 8–9

ABORTIONS WILL not let you forget.
You remember the children you got that you did not get . . .
If I stole your births and your names,
Your straight baby tears and your games . . .
If I poisoned the beginnings of your breaths,
Believe me that even in my deliberateness
I was not deliberate . . . Anyhow you are dead,
Or, rather, instead, you were never made.
O what shall I say? How is the truth to be said?

GWENDOLYN BROOKS: *The Mother*

COITION, FRUITION – trust of conceiving,
Flesh of our flesh God's image receiving,
Transacting, invoking, in love's sweet embrace,
Our birthright in grace.
Or greatly with child in mindless defying,
Flesh from our flesh the image defiling,
Crudely distorting, coldly aborting,
Babes for the thwarting.

ANONYMOUS: *Great with Child*

ALMIGHTY GOD . . . to whom all our undesirings are known, all our secrets open, and from whom no treasons are hidden: by all that was depraved in intercourse . . . turn the bitterness of guilt among the partners towards the pardon that remakes our broken truth. Amen.

GOD KNOWS the pregnancy in every womb and every foetus in miscarriage or in maturing.

Surah of Thunder 8

GOD HAS not set two hearts in the one self of a man.

Surah of the Confederates 4

ONE OF his signs is that he has created partners in marriage to be yours from your own selves so that, dwelling with them, you might find rest, he having ordained a mutual tenderness and compassion, wherein truly there are signs for thoughtful people.

Surah of the Byzantines 21

HE CALLED his love frankly a mystery . . . He only knew that the sight and memory of her moved him deeply, touching the spring of all love and tenderness, all faith and courage within him . . . He created the mind he believed in out of his own which was large, unselfish, tender.

GEORGE ELIOT: *Adam Bede*

O LORD OUR God, traditions of long standing have read your world in patriarchal terms, made fathers, uncles, brothers binding guardians of the female will and person. A deep distrust of the capacity of men for chastity and honour enjoins the veiling of wives' and sisters' beauty.

We pray that we may reach and prove that integrity can keep the trust of personhood, both ways, free and pure and gentle, that the disciplines and benedictions of authentic love may be known among us in the joyful meaning of our creaturehood and the good purpose of your holy will. Amen.

THEIR LORD . . . took them to witness on their own souls, saying: 'Am I not your Lord?'

Surah of the High Vantage-Points 172

I N GOD'S Name be the course and the mooring. Embark.

Surah of Hud 41

GIVE US thy wisdom
More than ever before,
Now that our country
Has passed the door
To wider freedom.

Hold a people's hand
And give us thy heart,
So that every man lives in the land,
And holds dear the part
He must play,
To fulfil this day.

Give us thy glory,
In the days ahead,
O let our country be proud of its story
When we are dead.

GEORGE CAMPBELL: *Jamaica Constitution Day Poem*

R EMEMBER, O Lord, in thy mercy this people, and all
peoples, this land and every land.
Look graciously upon the youth in the venture of life's
prospect and upon the aged in the anchorage of days.

Remember those in the full tide of their affairs – rulers,
leaders, artists, teachers, doctors, captains of industry and
makers of science, and all whose well-being they carry in
their trust.

Remember in thy compassion all travellers and wayfarers,
all pilgrims and passengers, and every common man
preserve thou, in his going out and coming in, his living and
his dying, O merciful Lord. Amen.

I T IS as one soul he created you, and as one soul he gives you life.

Surah of Luqman 27

OUR BREAD and water are of one table:
The progeny of Adam are as a single soul.

MUHAMMAD IQBAL: *Javid Nama*

HOLY BE the white head of a negro,
Sacred be the black flax of a black child.
Holy be the golden down
That will stream in the waves of the wind
And will thin like dispersing cloud.
Holy be heads of Chinese hair,
Sea calm sea impersonal
Deep flowering of the mellow and traditional.
Heads of peoples fair
Bright shimmering from the riches of their species:
Heads of Indians
With feeling of distance and space and dusk:
Heads of wheaten gold,
Heads of peoples dark
So strong, so original,
All of the earth and the sun.

GEORGE CAMPBELL: *Holy*

S URELY YOU know that you are God's temple, where the Spirit of God dwells. Anyone who destroys God's temple will be himself destroyed by God. For the temple of God is holy, and that temple you are.

First Epistle to the Corinthians 3.16–17

L ORD, TEACH us to hallow our humanity in the hallowing of thy Name. Amen.

O MAN, WHO has beguiled you away from your kindly Lord, who created you and fashioned you, wrought you with such symmetry and ordered you as he willed the design?

Surah of the Cataclysm 6–8

H ERE, LORD, before you tonight are the bodies of sleeping men:

> The pure body of the tiny child,
> The soiled body of the prostitute,
> The vigorous body of the athlete,
> The exhausted body of the factory worker,
> The soft body of the playboy,
> The surfeited body of the rich man,
> The starved body of the poor man,
> The painful body of the injured man,
> The paralysed body of the cripple,
> All bodies, Lord, of all ages.

I offer them all to you, Lord, and ask you to bless them,
While they lie in silence, wrapped in your night.
Left by their sleeping souls,
They are there before your eyes, your own.
Tomorrow, shaken from their sleep,
They will have to resume their work.
May they be servants and not masters,
Welcoming homes and not prisons,
Temples of the living God and not tombs.
May these bodies be developed, purified, transfigured,
By those who dwell in them.

MICHEL QUOIST: *The Pornographic Magazine*

THEY CONCEAL themselves from men, but not from God. For he is with them the while they muse aloud with themselves by night in his despite. God is there encompassing all they do.

Whoever does evil and wrongs himself and then prays God's forgiveness will find that God is All-forgiving and All-merciful.

Surah of Women 108, 110

THE DROWSY street eyes me,
And the brick walls bid me refrain,
And I sense God, too, watching me,
The night and the lamp – they are noting me,
And the star – why does the star
Want to beckon me so
Just when I am falling into sordid shame?
What am I but a body-slave?
The shame is like poison in my frame:
I feel the toxic evil overpowering me.
'Tis not the murmuring of the night transporting me,
Nor am I inebriate in the whispering air,
Nor can I tax some bewitching humming in the
     moonlight,
That I sense my inmost self inside a shroud.

HILAL NAJI: *The Worshipper of the Flesh*

SELL NOT yourself at a little price, being so precious in God's eyes.

JALAL AL-DIN RUMI: *Discourses*

IN YOUR watchful compassion, Lord, guard and guide us. Amen.

Petition ↭ 109

H AVE WE not given him two eyes?

Surah of the Land 8

THANK YOU, Lord, for my eyes
   Windows open on the wide world . . .
May my look never be one of disappointment,
Disillusionment, despair;
But may it know how to admire, contemplate, adore.

May my gaze not soil the one it touches,
May it not disturb, but may it bring peace.
May it not sadden, but rather may it transmit joy.
May it not attract to hold captive,
But rather may it persuade others
To rise above themselves to you.

I give you my soul,
I give you my body,
I give you my eyes,
That, in looking at men, my brothers,
It may be you who look at them,
And you who beckon.

MICHEL QUOIST: *Eyes*

TELL ME, what have my eyes seen?
Why have they demented been?
Hot like the oven burn mine eyes.
Remembrance in them restless lies.
They went upon their obstinate way,
Where in their waiting troubles lay.

SHAH 'ABDUL LATIF: *Obstinate Eyes*

G OD BE in my eyes and in my looking.

O MAN, YOU are making your toilsome way unto your Lord, to find what you have wrought. Stage after stage you will surely ride.

Surah of the Rending 6, 19

THE SWAYING coach, for all its load,
    Runs lightly as it rocks:
Grey time goes driving down the road,
    Nor ever leaves the box.

We jump into the coach at dawn,
    Alert and fresh and free,
And holding broken bones in scorn,
    'Go on!' shout we.

By midday all is changed about,
    Our morning hearts are cool:
We fear the slow descents and shout:
    'Go slow! you fool!'

By dusk we're used to jolt and din,
    And when the light is gone
We sleep before we reach the inn,
    As time drives on.

ALEXANDER PUSHKIN: *The Coach of Life*

L ORD OF men, who givest life and bringest to death, thou art the beginning and the end, the First and the Last, unchanging in every scene.

Keep us this and every day, in the path of life. Grant us strength according to our time. Unite our days in one. Let thy compassion go before and follow after us, that in the entail of our lives we may find the proof of thy mercy. For unto thee is our becoming and our returning. Amen.

HE GIVES life and he makes to die and to him you shall be returned.

Surah of Jonah 57

SEE, THEY return; ah, see the tentative
　　Movements, and the slow feet,
　　The trouble in the pace and the uncertain
　　Wavering!

See, they return, one, and by one,
With fear, as half-awakened;
As if the snow should hesitate
And murmur in the wind, and half turn back.

EZRA POUND: *The Return*

FINALLY, THERE is the separation that is caused by death, that final parting . . . Here all tongues are baffled: the cord of every remedy is severed. No other course remains open but patient fortitude . . .

IBN HAZM: *The Ring of the Dove*

TO YOU, Lord, is entrusted all that we have and are – our salvation, our vocation, our daily work, our families, our life and our death. So at the end, Lord, our prayer is the sum of all desire and of all prayer. Take and receive, Lord, my whole freedom, my memory, my understanding and my whole will, all that I have and possess. From you it came, Lord, to you I offer it all again. All is yours, dispose of it entirely according to your will. Give me only your love and your grace, for that is enough.

KARL RAHNER: *Prayers for Meditation*

HOLY THE God of the angels:
    he has wrought the resurrection.
Holy the God of the prophets:
    he has wrought the redemption.
Holy the God of the apostles:
    he has wrought forgiveness.

Corpus Inscriptionum Latinarum

O GOD, have mercy on me when I die
And lie lonely in the grave,
And when I stand between your hands;
For I have been a stranger in the world.

Pilgrimage Prayers

O GOD, give him rest with the devout and the just,
In the place of the pasture of rest
And of refreshment, of waters in the paradise
Of delight, whence grief and pain and sighing have fled away.
Holy, holy, holy, Lord God of hosts,
Heaven and earth are full of your holy glory.

Egyptian Commendation, fifth century

MAY HE be with God,
May he be with the living God,
May he be with the immortal God,
May he be in the righteousness of God,
May he be in the hands of God,
May he be in the great Name of God,
May he be where God's greatness is,
May he live in God, now and in the day
Of judgment, and in the eternal life of heaven.

Monumenta Ecclesiae Liturgica

G OD BE at my end and at my departing.

LORD GOD, here is a new creation. Open it to me in thy obedience and close it for me in thy forgiveness and thy favour. Provide for me herein a goodness thou mayest find acceptable at my hands. Let it be to me pure and prosperous and whatsoever of evil I do in it do thou pardon me therein, for thou art ever forgiving and merciful, loving and kindly.

ABU HAMID AL-GHAZALI: *Morning Prayer of Abraham*

KEEP ME in thy love
As thou wouldest that all should be kept in mine.
May everything in this my being
Be directed to thy glory
And may I never despair.
For I am under thy hand,
And in thee is all power and goodness.

DAG HAMMARSKJÖLD: *Markings*

BE THOU my vision, O Lord of my heart:
Nought be all else to me save that thou art,
Thou my whole thought, by day or by night,
Waking or sleeping, thy presence my light.

Be thou my wisdom, thou my true word,
I ever with thee and thou with me, Lord . . .
Thou and thou only first in my heart,
High King of Heaven, my treasure thou art.
Heart of my own heart, whatever befall,
Still be my vision, O Ruler of all.

Ancient Irish prayer

LORD OUR God, to thee does man call in the day of his need: thee does he thank in times of joy. Thou art everywhere present. Thou art near where thy community is gathered together.

Some perhaps flying from heavy thoughts, or followed by heavy thoughts. But some, too, coming from a quiet life of contentment and some perhaps with a satisfied longing hidden in a thankful heart enveloped in joyous thoughts.

Yet all drawn by the desire to seek God, the Friend of the thankful in blessed trust, the consolation of the weak in strengthening communion, the refuge of the anxious in secret comfort . . .

So let thy self be found in this hour . . . that the happy may find courage to rejoice at thy good gifts, that the sorrowful may find courage to accept thy perfect gifts.

For to men there is a difference in these things, the difference of joy and sorrow. But for thee, O Lord, there is no difference: everything that comes from thee is a good and perfect gift.

SØREN KIERKEGAARD: *Prayers*

PETITIONS TERMINATE in the presence of his bounty: needs fade away as the soul finds her reliance in himself. The need of the creature is not satisfied by the whole of created things. Rather his infinite longing demands to be met by infinite graciousness and power, by none other than the truth himself, praised and exalted be he.

FAKHR AL-DIN AL-RAZI: *The Clear and the Shining*

POSTSCRIPT

A PART IN COMMON PRAYER
DISCUSSED

THE PREFACE promised occasion to face the sundry questions that browsers or readers will bring to all the foregoing. Those who are contented need read no further: the discontented, however, will be many and will come well primed. There is no *Tasliyah* here, the Muslim will say, no salutation on Muhammad, no 'calling down of blessing' with mention of his name, as the Qur'an commands. Its omission must render the whole unusable by Muslims. Further, a Christian will enquire: Where is the threefold Name here, 'Father, Son and Holy Spirit'? How, lacking this, can any prayer be 'Christian'? Is there not some conspiracy of silence that nothing concludes with the due formula: 'Through Jesus Christ our Lord'? How can Christians come to God on any other ground? There must be something wilful, culpable, intolerable in such omission. Does it not amount to an unwarranted, guilty suppression, an utter disloyalty in no way to be condoned? The 'something understood' to have prayer right for either of the separate loyalties here in view may be far to seek. The whole exercise must be reproved. There is no case it can pretend to make which is not condemned in the making. What it might invoke can only spell betrayal, either way. True Muslims have as little warrant here as honest Christians. Let them stay apart and only so keep faith.

'Let patience have her perfect work', James the Apostle once wrote – and he no stranger to controversy (James 1.4). Let us defer query for the moment and consider why this book should want to broach such problems as doctrines set for it.

What is clear is that there is a growing awareness of pluralism. Its constraints are recognized on every hand. Our global humanity is compelled by technology and the media revolution to reconcile a 'one-world' reality with one which is still, culturally, intensely local, thanks to poverty, disease, privation and the 'need for roots'. Tourism is a cult of the privileged, yet wherever it alights it creates perceptions of disparity, idly glimpsed or bitterly resented. What is new now about human diversity is the moral challenge it brings, the pervasive malaise and the chronic injustice. No separate religion can enjoy immunity from problems common to them all in society, in the world economy, in the strife of nationalisms and the ethnic dimensions of human neighbourhood.

Moreover, the time has passed when any one faith, presuming to be 'the world's religion', can pretend to suffice every culture or dominate the future with isolated self-sufficiency. This, both Christians and Muslims will want to insist, does not call into question their worldwide relevance. But mission or vocation in such worldwide terms has to know that issues of war and peace, world economics, genetics, ecology, population, space ambitions and international laws of human rights, are in no exclusive competence. They demand the mind and will of religions in the plural. They concern the sundry irreligions of secular humanity.

We do not know this situation for what it is if we do not allow that faiths have to find at least some modest communion in what it demands. The same factors which have conduced to dialogue about beliefs surely point towards something common in responsive prayer to take us beyond mere debate on means and ends. We are all immersed in the same features of contemporary life. Techniques, from medicine to engineering, genetics and statistics, are the same for us all. The sciences are neutral from culture to culture and from faith to faith. Computers, cybernetics, cloning body parts, the Internet – these do not discriminate between religions. For practitioners there is a common community of skill and expertise. It must surely follow that in manipulating the same technology they are invited into similar moral and spiritual liabilities for its guidance and control. Do not such liabilities lead them back into religious frames of reference? How, then, can these liabilities be exempt from what prompts prayer?

This points away from the traditional segregation of devotional practice. It suggests an obligation to find how the physical bearings of a shared technology belong with personal faith and draw spiritual direction from it. Then there are all the occasions of civic and professional activity in hospitals, schools, universities and local communities where common prayer might have due place in the quest for sanity, discernment and courage. Issues that tax our patience and try our spirits are precisely where prayer is most expedient.

But what of the compromises – if such we see them to be – in which any such commonalty on our part will be involved? Are not doctrine, history, loyalty all against the idea? Have we any valid hope of proving legitimate in the venture?

The surest ground for confidence – as already hinted – is that the pages here needed no inventing. They did not have to be researched: they presented themselves even to initially casual notice – notice of such a sort as to grow into conviction. Compatibilities attested themselves, even in the context of things sharply antithetical.

One striking example is the convergence of the opening of the Christian *Te Deum Laudamus* and Islam's *al-Fatihah*, the 'Opener' of the Qur'an: *iyyaka na'bud wa iyyaka nasta'in*. Both the grammars, Latin and Arabic, are employing the emphatic pronoun in the same sense and for the same reason. The *Fatihah* does not say (as it might): *na'buduka*, 'we worship thee' – a normal attached pronoun. It adopts a deliberately insistent shape by employing *iyya* to which to attach a verb-preceding pronoun: 'Thee, thee only'. What the Latin does is precisely the same, though the familiar English forfeits it in the prosaic 'We praise thee, O God', rather than: 'Thee, being God, we praise'.

No conscious case for the Arabic being derived from the Latin is implied. It is simply the coincidence of usage that signifies. Postponing the trouble we are in when we reach 'the Father Everlasting', it is fair to say that this profoundly Christian hymn in its first and its final eight verses ('worship, govern, magnify, keep, have mercy, lighten, trust' – with 'the heavens and all the powers therein') has a fervently Muslim feel. If we must halt at the disparities – as we surely do – we cannot have them in disregard of what conjoins.

It is believed here that this affinity in a classic case may symbolize a certain kinship in praise, penitence and petition, as here made articulate from both sources, and that its significance may avail for common prayer. Has the searching self-reproach of a Hamid al-Ghazali altogether no kinship with the mental turmoil of a Francis Thompson, or the public conscience of the cordwainer al-Hallaj no converse with the private self of a Dag Hammarskjöld? What is not in doubt here is that the numerous citations from the Qur'an – with which most Christians are not conversant – kindle sympathies of heart around gratitude, awareness of nature, and the precarious mysteries of our human environment, our sexuality, parenthood and sense perceptions.

Only when so much is conceded do we really come to what might give us pause. To have no place for empathy would be to have no occasion for misgiving, for we would simply be imprisoned in exclusivism and ignoring those situations of common responsiveness in daily life.

But, with all the will in the world, are not the irreconcilables of Islam and Christ quite insuperable, quite nugatory of common spirituality, void of all but a fantasy of shared devotion? There will be those, in either camp, who hold so. The faiths are too far apart for any to have anything in common with one another. Things contrary are too massive between them. That is claimed to be the verdict of the centuries. Islam is too tenacious of its identity, its finality, its utter suitedness – by divine decree – to forgetful human nature, to accept the implications that wait on 'common prayer'. Some Christians, likewise, will be strenuously repudiating Islam even while protesting that they must 'love Muslims'. Such will not let the 'love' interrogate the 'repudiation'. Others will not even stay for the scruples of 'love' but make their anathemas complete. Surely, they will say, the finality of 'God in Christ' is decisively against any positive significance in a subsequent religion. Moreover, Muslims see the Incarnation as utterly derogatory to the exaltedness of Allah, while the Qur'an seems to disavow conclusively the cross of Jesus as actual or redemptive. It must follow that all else distinctively Christian – the Holy Spirit, the Church, the sacraments and the New Testament writings – are vetoed. What remains from which to extend the ventures of a self-cancelling quest for community?

Taking due measures of how formidable the dissuasives are, perhaps we can focus what is at stake about any 'part in common prayer' by noting the absence throughout this anthology of the familiar words: 'through Jesus Christ our Lord'. What of such a conspiracy of silence? Is not that formula crucial for any and every loyal Christian at prayer? How and why ever forsake it?

But is it forsaken in alternatives like: 'for thy Name's sake', or 'in thy merciful Name'? Formally, yes, but essentially, no. Christians come to God always on the ground of whom they believe God to be. 'He who has the Son has the Father also', seeing that 'from the Father's being-in-giving we have the Son': so the Johannine Letters, in line with the New Testament Gospels. On Christian lips, those alternative phrases carry that Christic trust. Why not, then, have it articulate and explicit? In order to make viable a community of potential prayer with others who lack yet, or always, that Christ-clue, but nevertheless instinctively invoke 'the Name of God'. What perhaps we may – for the time being – think of as the elasticity of the Name of God carries us both, while for the Christian, the Christian dimensions of that Name are for ever in control. Others, however, have not been made passengers in an act of prayer whose explicitness excluded them from being party.

All respect to those who insist the gesture here is wrong: all hope from those who find it rightly mediatorial if it enables them to be part of something common. Is there a proper patience in having a form of words in conscious abeyance, given that there is no foregoing of their meaning? What of – as we term it – 'the Lord's Prayer' itself in relation to the Creed's Christology? The parties will be tacitly 'apart' from their separate completeness in bringing together what is partial for them both. Does a faith always have to assert its own recognizances before it will relate beyond itself or may there be a right humility in a certain self-abnegation as the very form of ministry?

Clearly there will always be those who think not. They will be right unless the vocation is perceived as such. The place for dogma is not always prior in the things of the Spirit. Nor are faiths necessarily most loyal when they are most assertive. What matters is to read 'the mind of Christ', the Christ who was no stranger to controversy yet perceived potential where the right credentials were hidden from normal sight.

And as for traditional controversy between mosque and church, Qur'an and Gospel, need it be as obdurate as we have long supposed? A mere postscript is no place for an exhaustive exploration of what sunders. The task has been attempted elsewhere. Let it suffice here to ponder a vital clue in Islamic *du'a'* and join it to the central implication of the *Bismillah*, or Invocation of *Al-Rahman al-Rahim*, 'the merciful Lord of mercy'. The clue is the way in which Muslim devotion can make the plea of 'the Names' the entire gist of the prayer. Saying: *Ya Latif*, 'O thou kindly One', intending this or that circumstance yearning for 'kindliness', needs no elaboration, no further wordage. God is being invoked to be who he is by virtue of that Name. This calls for no tedious elaboration. He knows well enough how to be himself, and be so vis-à-vis what the pleader has in view.

Hence the admirable brevity of Islamic *du'a'*. It has a certain kinship with the brevity of the most chaste Prayer Book collects, where the theme of adoration is the requisite of the petition, so that ascription of praise and plea of soul are in unison. Examples are here, notably from *Hirz al-Jawshan*. The praying self is cast wholly on divine resources. To these the very 'Nameability' of God is the key.

Here we come upon a significance that surely embraces both the Muslim approach to Allah and a Christian's Christology. This Nameability entails, in some vital sense, a divine–human relation. God is known, describable and addressable, in human terms. To be sure, the orthodox Muslim theologians had great unease in conceding this, thanks to their intense preoccupation (for the sake of excluding idolatry) with exalting Allah far beyond all human language and the human characterization it implied. 'Exalted be He above all that you associate' was their incessant cry. Thus, in naming Allah they needed to deny that they were significantly doing so.

The dilemma can only be overcome by perceiving that the very transcendence of God admits, contains, includes, this describability. Doubtless the transcendent transcends all that connotes, but does so without cancelling that connotation. Otherwise, it is not only all theology and all faith that are annulled: it is also all worship and all prayer. For if we cannot veritably 'call' God we cannot 'call upon' him. Worship has to go – with theology – into the impenetrable silences and that is the end of Islam.

'His (literally, 'to him') are the adorable Names: so call upon him by them', says Surah 17.110. That is – in one – the trust of faith and the urge of worship, the affirmative/imperative of Muslim life. God, in His grace, condescends to the realm of human language and – doing so – underwrites a theology in the very context of enjoining and evoking worship. Such condescending into humanness in that compassionate sense is not such as to be somehow vetoed, queried or disavowed, as if to safeguard a divine unity that it put in jeopardy. For it was that very unity from within which the compassion came, which was – in any and every event – its own safeguard.

Through the divine Names in Islam Allah is invoked as the One who condescends to human language. How near, then, by these lights, to 'the Word made flesh' to 'dwell among us that we might behold his glory'? What is Christology but the Self-naming of God presented in human history as 'truth through personality' – and that personality in inclusively relevant human situations of dark suffering and redemptive love? To understand the Incarnation in its real dimensions is to learn the 'Nameability' of God as having stooped (as in 'the adorable Names') not only into human adjectives but into human 'life-in-writing'. Unyielding minds may protest it cannot be so, Allah being too remotely great, though the divine Names insist that only in *not* being remote is the greatness ever known. It might follow that to 'magnify' God truly is to find remoteness ever more disqualified. Both happen in 'the acknowledgement of God in Christ'. This must be the sufficient rationale for any present will to bring into some active and mutual expression the Muslim practice of the divine Names and the Christian measure of 'the Word made flesh'.

The most frequent pairing of the divine Names – the two in the Islamic *Bismillah* – may be seen to enshrine the same clue. For the words *Al-Rahman al-Rahim* have one R H M root but they are not mere repetition. There is a clear progression of meaning in the two derivatives: *Al-Rahman* denoting divine mercy as a quality-in-being *qua* essential nature, while *al-Rahim* indicates that quality in action, at work in fulfilling operation. If we – English-wise – reverse the order we have 'The merciful (*Rahim*) Lord of mercy (*Rahman*)'. The frequent English translation: 'The merciful, the compassionate' only partly captures the progressive idea of the grammar, and there must be a query around 'compassionate' for Muslims if the word really means 'to suffer with'.

In brief here, the vital point is that 'who Allah is' and 'how Allah relates' belongs in one. For Christians, it is in 'God in Christ' that this oneness in 'being-in-doing' most inclusively happens. For their own reasons (which we need to share as issues) Muslims will not normally allow this. Even so, in the 'space' of their own *Bismillah* it is possible to set the whole significance of what Christians know as Christology – the theme, central to faith, of that about God which is told in that about Christ and these, like the *Bismillah*, in an inner sequence prompting us to 'the knowledge and love of God'. All else in these pages may be said to follow from this.

'From Senegal to Samarkand' is no more than a poetic way of saying 'from West to East'. Extracts here from Léopold Senghor, Senegal's Christian president for a quarter-century, may serve for a west as far westwards as the Caribbean. The prayers of al-Dirini and of the Naqshabandi devout certainly reached beyond the famed city of Samarkand, a name to join Asia with the Atlantic and the Moroccan Atlas mountains where fellow Sufis had their kindred *zawiyas* (devotional groups at prayer).

Sources that are so evidently personal will lend themselves more readily to private than to corporate use. The intention is rather meditative than liturgical. Even so, the anthology may prove useful in school assemblies or on occasions of shared worship elsewhere, or in the context of informal dialogue where a concluding (or opening) focus of worship is desired.

The Christian tradition of 'biddings', whether in gratitude or intercession, finds ready parallel with the Muslim practice of *dhikr*, or 'recollecting' the divine presence in context. A 'bidding' can 'do' precisely what 'recall' of a 'Name' intends – the thought of God and the plea from the soul, in either order. *Hirz al-Jawshan*, for example, with a 'O Thou encompassing all', is phrasing both devotion and desire. God is being sought, for his own sake and for the sake of his own power and grace. If we have the will to greet it, we can surely sense the affinity that can exist between *du'a'* and litany.

The sections of Praise, Penitence and Petition justify themselves. All three terms are central to both religions. The sundry Quranic doxologies and celebrations of mercy in external nature and human society are apt enough for Christian use. The Qur'an's urging on Muslims of 'seeking forgiveness from God' is in line with that scripture's realism about the reach of human wrong, the callous inhumanity of humans, despite those aspects of the human scene being seen as more sanguine than a radical Christianity can allow. Where – as often – Muslim repentance is overly couched in 'fear of the Fire' and minatory 'frowns' in that scripture, these have been omitted, the better to concentrate on the inwardness and sincerity of self-reproach – qualities in no way lacking among Sufis, in a riper sense of 'the fear of the Lord'.

The pages of Petition are meant to kindle a sense of things for which prayer becomes inwardly alerted by imagination as minds in art and literature might shape it. Thus the epistolary greetings of Abu-al 'Ala al-Ma'ari suggest a temper of recollection that translates into taking our own absent friends into the divine presence. If prayer is well defined as 'joining with the work of love in the world', then what that work entails and where it is being pursued in public affairs and private realms become its liability. Where literature has drawn the scene, whether in wistfulness or despair, the will to pray can take its impetus.

The Qur'an, for example, shows a persistent interest in the womb, in birth as the threshold of temporal being, and in human intercourse as the crowning instance of divine trust. That register around the human embryo, its mystery and crisis, bears strongly on our responding solicitude concerning infidelity, contrived miscarriage, the psychic trauma of the aborting, the reproach and the redemption. All these belong with 'caring about love in the world' and we cannot do so without both the accusation and the overcoming in grace.

Petition, too, has to dwell where the needs press – the injustice of 'law's delays' and denials, the homelessness of the refugee, the anxieties of poverty and the blandishments of power. In all the spheres of human urgency, we must find the aspiration that disallows indifference and ventures active expectation. All these the psalmist meant by his 'waiting on the Lord'. The 'waiting' word suggests not only the hopeful on the lookout but the servant at the ready. In that sense petitionary prayer can energize its cares towards their due fulfilment, so that to pray is not to indulge – as otherwise it might be – in a ritual of exoneration, an escape into mere words.

It is intriguing that the Islamic call to *Salat*, the summons to the ritual prayer-rite, uses the verbal imperative *Hayya*, which might be translated: 'Look alive!' or 'Liven ye!' It is precisely this sense of life, in all its vagaries and imponderables, its tragedies and its benedictions, that petition at its truest is obeying. Penitence is thus bound to be its correlative. For all wrongs in society need to be, in some sense, acknowledged as our own, if we can understand how a presumed innocence can be itself a guilty haven. This is not to be morbidly inauthentic; it is rather to realize that there can be a will to vicariousness when we perceive the devious workings of the inhumanity to which we belong and – in the Qur'an's words – 'what the bosoms of men conceal'.

Comparably, the themes of gratefulness are so evidently shareable. When the Qur'an-reader celebrates the dawn and the fall of night, the rising of the moon and its crescent beauty, the freshening rains and the enduring oasis, there is something participatory as human and not only Islamic. The Biblical text, in psalm and prophet, is no less busy with doxology. There is always something reciprocal between meeting and meaning. To will the former is mutually to embrace the latter. The formula is reversible in that shared meaning fuses relationship. All the more crucial is this possibility, given the sharp and deep dissonances that echo in our histories. Where necessary controversy has fostered alienation, there is the greater reason to allow affinities also to assert themselves.

That case is strengthened when we realize that the range of religious vocabulary, the language of prayer, is not limitless. For the fecundity of nature and society in yielding imagery and metaphor by which words work, rich and inventive as it is, admits of no cultural monopoly. Thus it follows that many words and themes recur between religions – light, door, tree, water, lamp, bosom, glory – so that a certain literal kinship exists through all the range of meaning they intend. If not always community, at least elucidation, will relate the users.

Furthermore, inside the broad denominators 'Muslim' and 'Christian', there are wide differences as to how their terms are read, their vocabularies received. In neither faith are believers unanimous about how they take their confessional meanings. Even, from time to time, within their own individual experience and privacy of mind, they have unresolved issues of integrity. May not that situation suggest a livelier, more open, patience with each other? When 'congregation' – Muslim or Christian – means a certain mental 'segregation' (and no faith-system is unanimous), miscellaneous 'wholes', as Islam and Christianity purport to be, may the better reckon with each other in the issues their diversities acknowledge. So long as we are cognisant of tension and scrupulous about honesty of mind, the conscious sharing of vocabulary may itself stimulate these qualities. To find a partial consensus in prayer is to give what continues to divide a different temper and a wiser reckoning.

Take from the preface the two examples of how what we each forego in venturing partially common prayer may in fact be more reflectively present for each us by being held in abeyance. The one example is Muslim, the other Christian. In this collection Muslims find no *Tasliyah*, no salutation of

Muhammad – an obligation laid on Muslims by Surah 33.56. By the 'greeting' of the Prophet they celebrate his role in the economy of God, his status as the final messenger of Allah. That perception is integral to Islam alone. Christian exemption from its use, however, means no negation of the centrality to that economy which Muslims intensely hold, nor of their sincerity in doing so. It is an exemption which has two points. It sees something cognate to Christology in the Quranic concept of how 'Allah and his angels' 'find satisfaction' in the personhood of Muhammad, but it has already located in Jesus and his cross what is cognate, namely the divine kindredly engaged with the human, as Lord with servant, sovereignty with agency. Christology is alien to Islam in affirming incarnation. Yet the *Tasliyah* involves Islam, via the 'celebration' of Muhammad, in vital salutation of divine agency in the human. Christian abstention from *Tasliyah* can appreciate its Muslim intention only too well.

What Christians do not find in these pages is the explicit Holy Trinity. That central doctrine they, for their part, hold in abeyance. But, as with the Muslim forebearing about *Tasliyah*, doing so may serve a discovery of the meaning which 'Holy, Holy, Holy' affirms. The doctrine was never first a formula: it was an experience. Community between Christian and Muslim, if we can reach it in pages like these, will initiate us into precisely those dimensions of power, pardon and presence, a threefoldness in God, responsive to the yearnings and bearings of the humanity we share. If so, that result will be a surer acknowledgement of 'Father, Son and Holy Spirit' than any recital of the words. The questing hope for comprehension has to take over the fear of compromise.

In the words of the title suggested in the preface, 'A Part in Common Prayer', then, is 'apart' – as all prayer must be – in the sense of a shut door and a hallowed space. Here it has only been part of a consciously larger realm of worship, doctrine, tradition and liturgy. It can only be 'a part', too, of the historical and contemporary communities that are heir to those antecedent determinants by which they have endured. 'Parts', whether in drama or in life, are only so by dint of 'wholes'. Yet parts have not seldom been on behalf of wholes in ways that were vicarious towards the future. Initiatives do not have to be unanimous in order to be salutary. The wholes have other 'parts' and 'parties', the more raucous the more ambitious to be monopolist. In being forebearing with one another we also have to be wisely forebearing in our practice of authority and our discipline of belief.

Let these pages, then, be no more than a gesture of expectancy and an attempt to show its warrant. We have left conventional controversies aside, not in negligence of their import but in better hope of their resolution. Those minded to veto the whole will doubtless do so. 'He who judges is the Lord', theirs and ours.

'New room for others to turn about in' was how Eldridge Cleaver of the Black Panther party in the USA described the impact on him of the conversion of Malcolm X, after pilgrimage to Mecca. He turned from the hate-philosophy of the original Black Islam to hope of human community transcending racism. He greeted the uprising of white youth against social forms of white supremacy. It was only, as he said, 'a tiny place', but it was one in which he could 'attempt a manoeuvre of my own'. Such examples can be contagious. 'Room to turn in' – the inner meaning of *metanoia* – is what 'parties to common prayer' may afford to one another.

NOTES ON AUTHORS

As I have drawn on obscurity as well as fame, these paragraphs are not inclusive. Other names will be found in the index. Dates of Muslims are given here according to the Islamic calendar which begins in AD 622 with Muhammad's emigration from Mecca to Medina, which was 'the year of the Hijrah', or *Anno Hegirae*, hence the letters AH. To facilitate recognition for those unfamiliar with the Hijrah calendar the Western century is added in brackets.

SALAH 'ABD AL-SABUR, AH 1347–1401 (twentieth century)

Egyptian poet and playwright who consciously modelled his verse play *Ma'sat al-Hallaj* on T. S. Eliot's *Murder in the Cathedral*. His autobiography *My Life in Poetry*, explores the Eliot influence. His poems include the grief of Palestinians.

SHAH 'ABDUL LATIF, AH 1091–1161 (eighteenth century)

A village poet and saint of Sindh, whose *Shahju Risalo* is highly esteemed in Sindhi Islam as a work of great literary power and religious authority. He drew on the popular stories of local minstrels and transformed them into the vehicles of spiritual parable and praise.

LANCELOT ANDREWES, AD 1555–1626

Bishop of Winchester, England. His Latin book of personal devotions, *Preces Privatae*, was never intended for the public eye, but its ripe Biblical learning and warm fervour have enriched the prayers of many in the generations since his day.

AUGUSTINE OF HIPPO, AD 354–440

Great Christian saint, bishop and theologian, whose autobiography, *The Confessions*, is a classic of personal, spiritual revolution, the narrative of a man 'lost enough to be found' by faith. His *City of God*, his sermons and commentaries, deeply moulded Christian thought through the middle centuries.

LOUIS 'AWAD, AD 1914–1990

Egyptian critic, poet and novelist and, from the 1940s, a leading innovator in the use of the colloquial Arabic, against the grain of literary usage. His novel *al-'Anqa'* (*The Phoenix*) presents a metaphysics of socialism. He translated Horace's *Ars Poetica*.

'ABD AL-LATIF AL-BAGHDADI, AH 557–629 (twelfth/thirteenth centuries)

A most notable Islamic philosopher and scientist, who taught in Baghdad and travelled in Greece, Turkey, and Egypt. He was held in great esteem by Salah al-Din (Saladin), whose camp he joined outside Acre. He excelled in medical skill and his travelogue contains a graphic description of plague in Cairo.

MUSTAFA AL-BAKRI, AH 1099–1162 (eighteenth century)

Born at Damascus in the year John Bunyan died in Bedford, al-Bakri lived in Ottoman Palestine and in Cairo and Istanbul. He was a government official and a practising Sufi. His first manual of prayers was composed in Jerusalem. Known as 'the ascetic traveller', his devotional writing was widely influential in the Arab world.

ABUBAKAR, TAFAWA BALEWA, AH 1331–1385 (twentieth century)

Born at Bauchi in northern Nigeria, a teacher and a statesman and first federal premier of Nigeria, he died at the hands of assassins in the coup of January 1966. His novel *Shaihu Umar* vividly depicts the Hausa world of seventy years ago, its single-minded piety and the harsh realities of trans-Saharan travel.

ALEXANDER A. BLOK, AD 1880–1921

A very prominent poet in his generation in Russia, his verses are laden with carnal emotion and mystical melody, representing what one admirer called 'the tragic tenor of the era'.

BOETHIUS, AD 480–524

Christian theologian and man of wide learning, of influential birth and high culture. His experience of false accusation and imprisonment indwells his most famous work *On the Consolations of Philosophy*, a rich and strongly cherished manual of soul-courage and patient piety. He was killed in 524 and held as a martyr.

THOMAS BRADWARDINE, c. AD 1290–1349

Linked by Geoffrey Chaucer (in *The Canterbury Tales*) with Augustine and Boethius, Bradwardine enjoyed great repute as a theologian before his election as Archbishop of Canterbury in 1349. He died within seven days of landing at Dover to take up his charge. The Black Death was raging in England when he crossed the Channel.

BERTOLT BRECHT, AD 1898–1956

German playwright with a strong revolutionary and didactic passion. In his plays he aims to preclude identification or sympathy with his characters on the part of the audience, in order to compel the spectators to reach a verdict about the miseries and paradoxes they witness, the empty conventions and social follies.

GWENDOLYN BROOKS, AD 1917–

A black poet, born in Kansas, who succeeded Carl Sandburg as Poet Laureate of Illinois. Her *Selected Poems* (1963) deal with themes of tenement life and social deprivation. She edited a half-yearly magazine, *The Black Position*.

JOHN BUNYAN, AD 1628–1688

Author of *The Pilgrim's Progress* and *Grace Abounding* and one of the finest, lowliest figures in English Christian tradition, a man of simple greatness, telling imagination, warm compassion and vivid speech. His place in literature is truly 'an exaltation of the humble and meek'.

ALBERT CAMUS, AD 1913–1960

A French Algerian novelist and playwright with a buoyant capacity for life, for sunshine and the senses, and a thorough-going quality of ultimate despair about it. His literary works reflect with great force and clarity of language the wretchedness and tragedy of the human condition, its hypocrisy, its pathos and its pointless, but still persistent, demand for meaning.

GEORGE CAMPBELL, AD 1916–

A Jamaican poet whose *First Poems* were published in Kingston in 1945, and a voice of sanity, gentleness and aspiration in the stresses and changes of the Caribbean world.

CLEMENT OF ROME, died c. AD 100

Bishop of Rome near the close of the first Christian century and author of the *Epistle to the Corinthians*, one of the important documents of the early Church after the writings of the New Testament. It has been conjectured that Clement is the person of that name to whom Paul refers in his *Epistle to the Philippians* (4.3).

ARTHUR HUGH CLOUGH, AD 1819–1861

An English poet, the favourite pupil at Rugby School of the famous Thomas Arnold, and a close friend of his son, Matthew, Clough's poems reflect the alert, and often burdened, spirit with which he sensed and satirized the hypocrisies of his time.

WILLIAM COWPER, AD 1731–1800

Son of a priest and trained as a lawyer, he suffered acute self-doubt and at length found equanimity in quiet rural pursuits at Olney, where he wrote famous hymns, which he celebrated in a long narrative poem, *The Task*. 'A stricken Deer', he learned – at length – what Muslims call *itmi'nan*, 'tranquillity'.

STEPHEN CRANE, AD 1871–1900

The son of a Methodist minister in New Jersey, Crane struggled with poverty and ill-health as a journalist in New York, and as a war correspondent. He settled in England but illness, stemming from his privations, cut short his life. Dying before the age of thirty, he left stories and poems with a grimly realist quality of pathos and irony.

THOMAS CRANMER, AD 1489–1556

A scholarly figure, oddly yet heroically present at the centre of the stage through the tumult of the English Reformation. His external career as Archbishop of Canterbury ended in broken-ness and despair in the reign of Mary, but finding God again beyond the God he had lost, he recanted his recantation and in death gave to the English Church a sign of courage as hauntingly eloquent as his English *Litany*.

RICHARD CRASHAW, c. AD 1613–1649

Religious poet of seventeenth-century England, born of Puritan stock and converted to the Roman Catholic Church some few years before his death. He wrote sacred verse in both English and Latin, with an artistry of phrase and fervour of devotion unex-celled in an age of deep religious feelings and political passion.

'ABD AL-'AZIZ AL-DIRINI, died c. AH 697 (thirteenth century)

A celebrated poet and Sufi master who lived in rural Egypt and commented on the Qur'an, notably the *Fatihah*, and reputedly wrote a work with the title *Gathered Pearls on Assorted Questions*.

JOHN DONNE, AD 1572–1631

The most memorable English preacher of the seventeenth, and perhaps of any, century was first 'Jack' Donne, an amorous poet. The intensity of his religious experience, his sense of evil, of judg-ment and of death, his grasp on grace and redemption, were tuned to a fine and sombre eloquence by his wide erudition, his power of imagery and his probing wit. And still, because of him, 'love's mysteries in souls do grow'.

GEORGE ELIOT, (authorial name) AD 1819–1880

Born in the English Midlands as Mary Ann Evans, she forsook her early evangelical faith, influenced by the German philosopher Feuerbach, whom she translated into English. However, her influential novels had a warm, surviving, ethical fervour and she did not think of herself as a 'breeder of sceptics'. She was partnered, extra-maritally, by George Henry Lewes, who sponsored her publications.

FRANCIS OF ASSISI, AD 1181–1226

Son of a rich clothier in Assisi, Italy, Francis 'learned Christ' through a crisis of compassion in which he embraced poverty and found its positive meaning in active love and Gospel preaching. His repair of a ruined church became the symbol and the magnet of a discipleship which grew into the Franciscan Order. Seven years before his death he visited the Arab East. He lives in history in the 'sign' of the five wounds, the *Stigmata*.

ALEKSEI K. GASTEV, AD 1882–1941

One of a group of young proletarian poets in Russia who wrote ecstatically of the power of the machine and celebrated the promise of collectivism and new industrialization. He thought the universe a huge foundry.

PAULUS GERHARDT, c. AD 1607–1676

One of the finest poets of German Lutheran Christianity, who drew upon medieval sources and upon an ardent love of nature and sense of grace to give hymns of rich devotion to the music of Christian worship.

ABU HAMID MUHAMMAD AL-GHAZALI, AH 450–505 (eleventh century)

The most justly famous of spiritual leaders in Islam. While in his thirties and already a successful philosopher, he experienced a deep, personal crisis of conversion from pride and despair. His masterpiece, *Ihya' 'Ulum al-Din* (*The Reviving of the Sciences of Religion*), is a profound work of intellectual range and moral perception and embraces knowledge, evil, sin, temptation, discipline, sanctity, and hope, among its themes. Other numerous works gave wide currency to his legacy as a supreme exponent of Islamic existence.

HUGO GROTIUS, AD 1583–1645

Eminent Dutch jurisprudent, pioneer of the concept of international law and ardent for Christian ecumenism and reunion. He lived through turbulent times but imprisonment did not daunt either his enormous talents or his vision. He was a European as versatile as Ibn Sina.

SHAMS AL-DIN HAFIZ, AH 720–791 (fourteenth century)

Foremost in the art of Persian *ghazal* poetry, Hafiz, born in Shiraz – the city of poets – and a Shi'ah Muslim (his name indicates that he had learned the Qur'an by heart), lived through chequered times. 'What is this anarchy that I see in the lunatic world?' he wrote. Beneath the dismaying tumults, his poems breathe a tranquillity of soul of which an English translator said: 'They are the plants and flowers of light; they toil not, neither do they spin, yet eternity is full of their glory.'

HAFSA OF GRANADA, c. AH 530–586 (twelfth century)

Celebrated poet in Spain in the days of the Almoravids, Hafsa Bint al-Hajj was a woman of great social charm whose Arabic verses were characterized by a simple directness and human sympathy. She lived through a devastating plague at Marrakesh, Morocco, which left a deep mark upon her courtly mind. She died there some years later.

DAG HAMMARSKJÖLD, AD 1905–1961

'A man of true inner greatness in a position of high leadership . . . sustained and inspired by pure and firmly founded beliefs and ideals about life and relationships . . . a very brilliant, orderly, pragmatic and subtle mind' (quoted from the introduction to Dag Hammarskjöld, *The Servant of Peace: A Selection of his Speeches*, ed. W. Foote, London, 1962, pp. 13–14). Second Secretary-General of the United Nations, a man of peace and prayer.

AMIR HAMZAH, AH 1329–1365 (twentieth century)

A Malayan prince, writing in Bahasa Indonesian, his poems breathe a deep wistfulness for human love and speak an ardent Muslim devotion. His two volumes of verse were *Songs of Loneliness* and *Fruits of Longing*. He edited other poems called *License from the East* and was fluent in Persian, Urdu, and Turkish. He was killed by revolutionaries in Sumatra.

ABU MUHAMMAD 'ALI IBN HAZM, AH 384–456 (eleventh century)

Celebrated theologian and legist of Cordoba and a doughty con-troversialist who lived through turbulent times of political unrest and confronted them with a sharp prolific pen. His trea-tise on the art and practice of love, *The Ring of the Dove*, is in quieter vein and remains one of the most fascinating literary legacies of Muslim Spain.

MARY HERBERT, COUNTESS OF PEMBROKE, AD 1561–1621

One of the literati of the Tudor/Stuart period, sister of Sir Philip Sidney and an editor of the metrical psalms.

JOHN S. HOYLAND, AD 1887–1957

A Christian educator who spent many years in India and laboured to interpret India to the West and Christ to India. He wrote the biographies of G. K. Gokhale and C. F. Andrews and translated Mahatma Gandhi's *Songs from Prison* into English. He also wrote *The Great Forerunner*, a study of the relation of Platonism to Christianity.

KAMEL HUSSEIN, AH 1320–1398 (twentieth century)

Cairo surgeon and educationalist, whose contemporary reflec-tions on the philosophy of religion, archaeology, psychology, and Arabic literature have found expression in essays and other works, notably *Qaryah Zalimah* (*City of Wrong*), a study of the motives and decisions leading up to the rejection of Jesus in the first century, as symptomatic of the whole range of evil in human society.

AHMAD IBN IDRIS, *d.* AH 1253 (early nineteenth century)

A noted Moroccan mystic who migrated, first to Cairo and then to Mecca, and attracted a large following of disciples. His theology hardened in his later years and he died in Asir, under the protection of the Wahhabi rulers. His influence survives among the Sanusiyyah of Libya and in the Sudan.

EUGENE IONESCO, AD 1912–1994

A dramatist of French Rumanian parentage who preached the evils of conformism and satirized, with sometimes witty and always mordant irony, what he considered to be the banalities of society, sex, and friendship, intimating his view of the emptiness and oppressiveness of the human scene.

MUHAMMAD IQBAL, AH 1294–1357 (twentieth century)

The greatest literary figure in twentieth-century Islam in Asia. His poems in Persian and Urdu contributed massively to the renewal of Muslim vitality in the subcontinent of India. He is revered by multitudes as the spiritual mainspring of Pakistan. He had a lively sympathy with such Western thinkers as Nietzsche, Shaw, and Bergson.

'ABD AL-QADIR AL-JILANI, AH 470–561 (twelfth century)

A distinguished jurist of the Hanbali School, who became a celebrated preacher, after an experience of Sufi illumination in Baghdad when he was almost fifty years of age. He originated the Qadiriyyah Order, which spread widely in western Asia, Egypt and, later, India. Its litanies and prayer manuals direct the devotional lives of initiates and 'lay' associates.

SØREN KIERKEGAARD, AD 1813–1855

One of the foremost influences from the nineteenth century in contemporary Christian thought. His early death symbolizes the strain of sadness which beset his family and his career. His incisive mind at length found its authentic 'word' in existential faith and in a passionate rejection of institutional religion. Nevertheless his meditations on 'Holy Communion' represent his most intense message to posterity in their discovery of grace.

HUGH LATIMER, c. AD 1485–1555

Bishop of Worcester, England, and, with Nicholas Ridley and Thomas Cranmer, the most famous martyr of the English Reformation. He was a forceful and lively preacher whose robust personality surmounted the pathos of his old age and his tragic end.

ABU-L-'ALA AL-MA'ARI, AH 363–449 (tenth/eleventh centuries)

A leading poet and thinker and one of the profoundest sceptics within Islam, a man with a wistful sense of the human tragedy. Blinded, scarred by smallpox, disillusioned with Baghdadi scholarship, he lived in seclusion near Aleppo and wrote poems, letters and imaginative works, and through his more than eighty years he defiantly endured, yet contrived also to grace, the human enigma.

MUHAMMAD AL-MAGHUT, AD 1934–

Syrian journalist, playwright and television dramatist, his *Diwans* register the lostness of 'the outsider', and capture the contemporary malaise of Arab experience.

CLAUDE MCKAY, AD 1889–1948

A poet of Jamaica and America who also made extended visits to France and Russia, knew the attraction of Communism but found no rest in its dogmatics. He wrote novels of the sordid city and gentle poems of affection for a Jamaica to which he never returned. 'Adventure-seasoned and storm-buffeted I shun all signs of anchorage.'

ALICE MEYNELL, AD 1847–1922

Essayist and publisher and, with her husband Wilfred, the rescuer of Francis Thompson (q.v.) from spiritual destitution into a quality of Christian experience – akin to her own – of deep and sacramental sense of 'God-in-Christ'.

'Iyad Ibn Musa, ah 476–544 (eleventh century)

Moroccan poet and historian, born at Ceuta, who became Qadi of Cordoba and died in Marrakesh. He wrote extensively in the field of Tradition and Malikite law.

The Naqshabandi Order

A group of Sufi fraternities, founded in Persia and Bukhara by Baha'al-Din Naqshabandi, who died in ah 791 (ad 1389). One of its characteristics is the practice of the recollection of God in the act of inhaling and exhaling of breath. Its liturgies contain a wealth of aspiration, contrition, and the seeking of divine forgiveness.

Ezra Pound, ad 1885–1972

An American poet with a troubled history of political and literary vagaries but no less, for that reason, a voice of contemporary humanity. His *Cantos* contain passages of haunting eloquence and passionate feeling.

Alexander S. Pushkin, ad 1799–1837

Russia's greatest poet, of partly Ethiopian descent, of which he was very proud. He lived and died in the society so vividly depicted later in Tolstoy's *War and Peace*. His untimely death only added to the appeal of his genius.

Michel Quoist, ad 1918–

A priest of the Roman Catholic Church whose *Prayers of Life* have had a wide circulation as a quickening example of reflective praying within the realities of the contemporary world.

Karl Rahner, ad 1904–1984

One of the most influential of contemporary theologians in the Roman Catholic Church, who contributed powerfully to an interpretation of the pastoral role of the Church, as well as to inter-religious relations of Christian faith in the secular situation. He became a Jesuit in 1922 and was Professor of Christian Thought at the University of Munich, Germany.

FAKHR AL-DIN RAZI, AH 543–606 (twelfth century)

Among the foremost of classical commentators on the Qur'an, a native of Rayy (Tehran), who wrote extensively in Islamic philosophy and theology and proved a prodigious champion of his Sunni faith. He travelled in Bukhara and beyond to India and died in Afghanistan. One of his largest works is a treatise on the divine Names.

JALAL AL-DIN RUMI, AH 604–671 (thirteenth century)

The greatest of the mystical poets of Persian Islam. Born at Balkh, he fled before the Mongol invasions to Baghdad and later to Konya in Turkey, where he became a master of Sufi devotion and wrote the *Mathnawi*, the supreme classic of the Mawlawiyyah Order and a work of spiritual genius. The devotional occasions of his Order utilize the *nay*, or musical flute, and the celebrated 'whirling' rhythm.

GEORGE WILLIAM RUSSELL, AD 1867–1935

Irish writer and revivalist, theorist of a traffic of spirit between India and the Celts, butt of the satire of the 'nihilist' Samuel Beckett, he wrestled with the Irishness of Ireland in all its complexity.

MUSLIH AL-DIN SA'DI, c. AH 615–691 (thirteenth century)

The Persian poet, whose *Bustan* and *Gulistan*, written in Shiraz, the home of poets, are the pride of Persian literature. Sa'di lived in the tragic century of Mongol expansion and the end of the 'Abbasid caliphate in the sack of Baghdad (AD 1258). He spent much of his life in seclusion. His work is sometimes commonplace and his prose anecdotal, but his lyrics have a superb quality of simplicity and grace.

LÉOPOLD SÉDAR SENGHOR, AD 1906–

Born in a coastal village in Senegal, West Africa, President of the Republic of Senegal until 1980 and one of the most expressive of African poets in the French language. He is a mainspring of the concept of *négritude*, and the positive assertion of the African identity, while being thoroughly alive in the European idiom. His poems, *Prayer for Peace* and *Paris under Snow*, accuse, forgive, and transcend the imperial wrongs.

CHRISTOPHER SMART, AD 1722–1771

A strange paradox of a man who lived a life of tragic sordidness, of debt, insanity, and literary jobwork and yet produced poems that are among the greatest in the lyrical, religious tradition of the English language, with an intensity of perception into nature and the skill of a miniaturist in words.

HENRY SUSO, c. AD 1295–1366

'Servant of the Eternal Wisdom', a man of German birth and a pupil of Meister Eckhart and a Dominican mystic, his meditations deeply influenced Thomas à Kempis in the *Imitation of Christ*.

GERHARDT TERSTEEGEN, AD 1697–1769

A notable hymn writer in the quietist tradition of German piety, who exercised a wide influence comparable to that of a Sufi *wali* in Islam in the fostering of spiritual devotion by a pattern of ascetic discipline. His community at Otterbeck formed the nucleus of his ideals and his poetry has been much translated.

FRANCIS THOMPSON, AD 1859–1907

Born in Lancashire, he fell into opium addiction and deep poverty, a derelict on the the streets of London. Sunk low in soul, his heart and his talents were retrieved by the Meynells (q.v.). His poetry expressed the depth of his soul-saga in a strangely powerful idiom.

AHMAD AL-TIJANI, AH 1150–1231 (eighteenth century)

A leading figure in North African Islamic religion, who studied at the great university at Fez, where he established the Sufi fraternity that spread throughout the Maghrib and the Sahara, as well as northern Nigeria and the Sudan. His prayer manuals have a still wider acceptance as a school of Muslim devotion.

THOMAS TRAHERNE, AD 1637–1674

Centuries of Meditations and the *Poems* reflect a rare quality of spiritual reverence and delight in divine mercy. The former remained in private manuscript for three hundred years and by its publication in 1908 one of the sweetest voices of the seventeenth century emerged to bless the twentieth.

ABU BAKR MUHAMMAD IBN TUFAYL, c. AH 505–581 (twelfth century)

A native of Granada, Spain, and an official of the Almohad court in Cordoba. His major work was a philosophical romance, in which a desert island 'Crusoe' ripened, as he grew in years, in the steady apprehension of rational truth, though entirely cut off from all human intercourse. When Islam reached his island he was convinced of its utter accord with philosophy. He initiated a mission to convert the world, but abandoned the venture to retire to his island sanctuary of pure belief and philosophic calm.

FYODOR I. TYUTCHEV, AD 1803–1873

A lyrical poet whose Russian verse, some in translation, has had a greater circulation since his death than in his own generation. His external success in the diplomatic and state service of the Czar makes a paradoxical background for a poetry that explores the dark areas of human experience.

HENRY VAUGHAN, AD 1621–1695

Born in Wales and educated at Jesus College, Oxford, practised in medicine, he emerged as a mystical poet, greatly influenced – via deep conversion – by the poems of George Herbert (q.v.).

With what he called 'my gazing soul' his intuitive mind dwelled in 'shadows of eternity'.

Eric Milner White, AD 1884–1964

For many years Dean of York Minster, England, author of *My God, My Glory* and other writings of Christian devotion, who stands in a long tradition of the care of stone, of music and of poetry in the service of God's worship and praise.

Walt Whitman, AD 1819–1892

Poet of Long Island, New York, of warm human sympathies and eccentric ways, a lover of sea and soil and cities, a visionary capable of majestic poetic rhythms as well as of much sentimental egotism, he grew to become in reputation and in retrospect a voice of idealism and the American Dream.

William B. Yeats, AD 1885–1939

Dublin poet and dramatist, interpreter of Irish feeling and thought, often disillusioned with his native land but always capable of direct and vigorous expression, intense both in loves and hatreds.

Zuhair 'in the days of the *Jahiliyyah*' (seventh century)

One of the outstanding poets of the 'time of ignorance' as the period before the rise of Islam is traditionally called. The precise date of Zuhair and other singers, in relation to Islam, has been a matter of controversy, some scholars believing that their poems, as they now stand, bear evidence of Islamic influence. Whether wholly prior to the Prophet or not, they celebrate both the prowess and the tragedy of the feuding tribes.

SOURCES AND ACKNOWLEDGEMENTS

All passages quoted from the Qur'an and, unless otherwise indicated, those from other sources, are translated by the editor. Arabic sources not detailed are prayer manuals which exist in numerous editions, popularly reprinted in many cities, often without page numbering and usually undated. Prayers for which no source is given are by the editor. Grateful acknowledgement is made to publishers and copyright owners for the use of extracts from these works.

PRAISE

page

7   E. Milner White, *My God, My Glory* (London, SPCK, 1967), p. 112.

7   Jalal al-Din Rumi, *Discourses*, trans. A. J. Arberry (London, John Murray, 1961), p. 152.

8   Abu-l-Salt, 'Bounty', in *Moorish Poetry*, trans. A. J. Arberry (Cambridge, Cambridge University Press, 1953), p. 16.

9   Augustine, *Confessions*, I.i. trans. E. B. Pusey (London, Grant Richards, 1900), p. 1.

10   Karl Rahner, *Prayers for Meditation*, trans. Rosaleen Brennan (New York, Herder & Herder, 1968; London, Burns & Oates), p.12.

10   Thomas Traherne, 'Thanksgivings for the Body', in *Centuries, Poems, and Thanksgivings*, ed. H. M. Margoliouth (Oxford, Clarendon Press, 1958), vol. II, p. 228.

11   Rahman Baba, 'A Pushtu Poem', in *Presenting Pakistani Poetry*, trans. Muhammad Aziz Kahn, ed. G. Allama (Karachi, Pakistan Writers' Guild, 1961), pp. 124–5.

12   *Ramadan Prayers*, in *Mukhtasar Ad'iyat Ramadan* (Sidon, Lebanon, 1930).

13   Mustafa al-Bakri, 'Seal of the Five Prayers', trans. C. E.
      Padwick, in *Muslim Devotions* (Oxford, Oneworld
      Publications, 1996), p. 74.

13   Sa'di, *The Gulistan*, trans. Edward Rehatsek (London,
      Allen & Unwin, 1964), p. 57.

14   *Benedicite* (*Book of Common Prayer*, Morning Prayer,
      from Song of the Three Children [Apocrypha] verses
      35ff.; here quoted: 35, 53, 54, 60, 63, 65).

15   G. Tersteegen, 'Lo! God is here, let us adore', trans. John
      Wesley (*English Hymnal*, no. 637, and other books).

15   Amir Hamzah, 'One Alone', trans. A. H. Johns, in
      Malayan and Indonesian Studies, ed. John Bastin and R.
      Roolvink (London, Oxford University Press, 1964),
      pp. 318–19.

15   'Abd al-Qadir al-Jilani, 'Wells of Prayer', trans. C. E.
      Padwick, in *Muslim Devotions*, op. cit., p. 98.

16   Augustine, *Confessions*, X.vi, op. cit., p. 234.

16   Lancelot Andrewes, *Preces Privatae*, in *Lancelot
      Andrewes and his Private Devotions*, ed. Alexander Whyte
      (London, Oliphant, Anderson & Ferrier, 1896), p. 66.

17   *Apostolic Constitutions*, Book VIII, in *Early Christian
      Prayers*, trans. W. Mitchell, ed. Adalbert Hamman
      (London, Longmans, Green & Co., 1961), p. 105.

17   *Prayers of the Naqshabandi Order*.

18   Abu Hamid al-Ghazali, 'The Beginning of Guidance',
      trans. W. Montgomery Watt in *The Faith and Practice of
      al-Ghazali* (Oxford, Oneworld Publications, 1994),
      p. 113.

18   Lancelot Andrewes, *Preces Privatae*, in *Lancelot
      Andrewes and his Private Devotions*, op. cit., pp. 70–1.

19   *Apostolic Constitutions*, Book VIII, in *Early Christian
      Prayers*, op. cit., p. 113.

19   Hafsa of Granada, 'The Shield', in *Moorish Poetry*, trans.
      A. J. Arberry, op. cit., p. 94.

20   Thomas Bradwardine, Archbishop of Canterbury, tomb
      inscription, Canterbury Cathedral.

20   Abu Hamid al-Ghazali, 'The Beginning of Guidance',
      trans. W. Montgomery Watt in *The Faith and Practice of
      al-Ghazali*, op. cit., pp. 140–1.

20 Egyptian Christian papyrus, *Patrologia Latina*, 18:442, in *Early Christian Prayers*, op. cit., p. 94.

21 Ahmad ibn Idris, *Prayers*.

21 Henry Suso, 'The Exemplar', in *Life and Writings of the Blessed Henry Suso*, ed. Nicholas Heller, trans. M. A. Edward (Dubuque, Iowa, The Priory Press, 1962), vol. I, p. 25.

21 Lancelot Andrewes, *Preces Privatae,* in *Lancelot Andrewes and his Private Devotions*, op. cit., pp. 79–80.

22 Abu Hamid al-Ghazali, *Prayer of the Prophet Muhammad*, in *Majallat al-Azhar*, Ramadan AH 1387 (AD 1967), vol. XXXIX, no. 7.

23 Christopher Smart, 'On the Eternity of the Supreme Being', in *Collected Poems*, ed. N. Callan (London, Routledge & Kegan Paul, 1949), vol. I, pp. 227–30.

24 Henry Suso, 'The Exemplar', in *Life and Writings of the Blessed Henry Suso*, op. cit., vol. I, p. 25.

25 Ibid.

25 Thomas Traherne, 'Thanksgivings for the Body', in *Centuries, Poems, and Thanksgivings*, op. cit., vol II, pp. 218, 220, 221 (lines 143–52, 158–60, 242, 254–65).

26 'Abd al-Qadir al-Jilani, 'Wells of Prayer', in *Muslim Devotions*, op. cit., p. 254.

26 Ibn Hazm, *The Ring of the Dove*, trans. A. J. Arberry (London, Luzac & Co., 1953), p. 177.

27 John S. Hoyland, *The Fourfold Sacrament* (Cambridge, Heffer, 2nd edition, 1924), p. 67.

27 George Campbell, 'Litany', from *Caribbean Voices*, vol. I: *Dreams and Visions*, ed. H. John Figueroa (London, Evans Brothers, 1967), p. 27.

28 Henry Vaughan, 'Rules and Lessons', in *The Works of H. Vaughan*, ed. L. L. Martin (2nd edition, Oxford, Clarendon Press, 1957), p. 436.

28 Thomas Traherne, 'Amendment', in *Centuries, Poems, and Thanksgivings*, op. cit., vol. II, stanzas 4 and 6, p. 436.

29 Boethius, *Consolations of Philosophy*, Book 3, versified by Samuel Johnson (London, 1906).

29 William Cowper, *Poetical Works*, ed. W. Benham, (London, Macmillan & Co., 1889), p. 423.

29   George W. Russell, 'Prayer', in *Collected Poems* (London, Macmillan & Co., 1913), p. 22.

30   'Abd al-'Aziz al-Dirini, 'Purity of Heart', trans. C. E. Padwick, in *Muslim Devotions*, op. cit., p. 219.

30   Percy B. Shelley, *The Witch of Atlas*, stanzas LXI–LXII, in *The Complete Poetical Works of Percy Bysshe Shelley*, ed. Thomas Hutchinson (London, Oxford University Press, 1905), p. 379.

30   *The Book of Common Prayer*, The Third Collect at Evening Prayer.

31   John Milton, *Paradise Lost*, Book III, lines 60–3.

31   Paulus Gerhardt, *Hymn at Nightfall*, trans. 'Y. H.' (Robert Bridges in *Yattendon Hymnal*; v. 3 omitted by permission).

32   *Ramadan Prayers*, in *Mukhtasar Ad'iyat Ramadan* (Sidon, Lebanon, 1930).

32   *Patrologia Orientalis*, 24:670.

33   Invocations from *Hirz al-Jawshan*.

33   Abu-l-'Ala al-Ma'ari, *Poems*, trans. H. Baerlein (London, John Murray, 1914), no. 13, pp. 85–6.

33   Thomas Traherne, *Centuries, Poems, and Thanksgiving*, op. cit., vol. I, pp. 102, 104 (Second Century, 90, 92).

34   John Keats, *Poetical Works*, ed. H. W. Garrod (2nd Edition, Oxford, Clarendon Press, 1958), p. 475.

34   Alice Meynell, *The Poems* (London, Oxford University Press, 1940), p. 20.

35   'Abd al-Latif al-Baghdadi, *Kitab al-Ifadah wa-l-I'tibar* (Paris, 1810), pp. 152, 154.

36   Mary, Countess of Pembroke, British Museum, unpublished MS, ed. R. G. B. (London 1857).

PENITENCE

41   Invocations from *Hirz al-Jawshan*.

42   'Abd al-'Aziz al-Dirini, *Taharat al-Qulub* (Cairo, n.d.), p. 177.

42   Hebridean Altars, source unknown.

43   Lancelot Andrewes, *Preces Privatae*, in *Lancelot Andrewes and his Private Devotions*, op. cit., p. 143.

43   Dag Hammarskjöld, *Markings*, trans. Lief Sjöberg and

W. H. Auden (London, Faber & Faber, 1964), p. 176.

44   Abu Hamid al-Ghazali, *The Deliverer from Wandering, Al-Munqidh min al-Dalal* (Cairo, AH 1309), pp. 20–31.

44   Basil Dowling, 'As Others See Us', in *Signs and Wonders* (Caxton Press, Christchurch, New Zealand, 1945).

44   *The Book of Common Prayer*, The Collect for Purity, Holy Communion Service.

45   Jalal al-Din Rumi, *Mathnawi*, 'The Man who Looked Back on his Way to Hell', trans. R. A. Nicholson, in *Rumi, Poet and Mystic* (Oxford, Oneworld Publications, 1995), p. 56.

45   Lancelot Andrewes, *Preces Privatae*, in *Lancelot Andrewes and his Private Devotions*, op. cit., pp. 120–2.

46   *Prayers of the Naqshabandi Order*.

46   Abubakar Tafawa Balewa, *Shaihu Umar* (London, Longmans, Green & Co., 1967), p. 176.

47   *Pilgrimage Prayers, Manasik al-Hajj wa Ad'iyat-al-Tawaf* (Cairo, 1947).

47   Søren Kierkegaard, *Journals*, trans. and ed. A. Dru (London, Oxford University Press, 1938), p. 73.

47   Abu Hamid al-Ghazali, 'Prayer of Adam', in *The Reviving of Religion, Ihya 'Ulum al-Din* (Cairo edition, AH 1309), I, 9, p. 286.

47   Dag Hammarskjöld, *Markings*, op. cit., p. 178.

48   *Prayers of the Naqshabandi Order*.

49   Lancelot Andrewes, *Preces Privatae*, in *Lancelot Andrewes and his Private Devotions*, ed. F. E. Brightman (London, Methuen, 1903), p. 196.

49   Abu Hamid al-Ghazali, *The Reviving of Religion*, op. cit., I, 9, pp. 287–8.

50   Tradition noted by Ibn Hazm, *The Ring of the Dove*, op. cit., p. 281.

50   Stephen Crane, 'War is Kind', in *The Works of Stephen Crane*, ed. W. Follet (New York, Russell & Russell, 1895), vol. VI, p. 122, no. 12.

51   Hugh Latimer, *Sermons*, ed. John Watkins (1824), vol. I, p. 123.

51   Arthur Hugh Clough, 'The Latest Decalogue', in *Poetical Works*, ed. F. T. Palgrave (London, Routledge & Sons, 1906), p. 44.

52   Ezra Pound, First Pisan Canto, *The Pisan Cantos* (London, Faber & Faber, 1949), p. 7, lines 1–2.

52   Mufakrul-Islam, *Bengali Poems*.

53   Jalal al-Din Rumi, *Tales from the Mathnawi*, trans. A. J. Arberry (London, Allen & Unwin, 1961), p. 42.

54   Ahmad ibn Idris, *Prayers, Ahzab wa Awrad*.

54   Ahmad Bashaikh ibn Husain, 'Shairit waa baruwa', trans. Lyndon Harries, in *Swahili Poetry* (London, Oxford University Press, 1964), pp. 259–61 (stanzas 6–8).

55   John S. Hoyland, *The Fourfold Sacrament*, op. cit., p. 67.

55   *Pilgrimage Prayers*, op. cit.

55   Abu Hamid al-Ghazali, *The Reviving of Religion*, op. cit., I, 9, pp. 287–8.

57   Fyodor I. Tyutchev, in *Poems from the Russian*, trans. F. Cornford and E. P. Salaman (London, Faber & Faber, 1943), p. 46.

58   Shenute, *Coptic Prayers of Dair al-Abyad, Egypt, in Early Christian Prayers*, op, cit., pp. 191–2.

58   Amir Hamzah, 'In Darkness,' trans. A. H. Johns, in *Malayan and Indonesian Studies*, ed. John Bastin and R. Roolvink (Oxford, Clarendon Press, 1964), p. 319.

58   Invocations from *Hirz al-Jawshan*.

59   Ahmad al-Tijani, *Prayers*.

60   Albert Camus, *The Fall*, trans. Justin O'Brien (London, Heinemann, 1957), pp. 101, 103.

60   John Donne, 'Good Friday, Riding Westward', in *Poetical Works*, ed. H. J. C. Grierson (Oxford, Clarendon Press, 1912) vol. I, p. 337, lines 39–42.

PETITION

63   Invocations from *Hirz al-Jawshan*.

64   'Utendi wa Mwana Kupona', trans. Lyndon Harries, in *Swahili Poetry*, op. cit., pp. 73, 75, 85.

64   Abu Hamid al-Ghazali, *The Reviving of Religion*, op. cit.

65   Tradition of the Prophet, noted by Muslim and Ibn Khaldun. See *Al-Muqaddimah*, ed. F. Rosenthal (London, Routledge & Kegan Paul, 1958), vol. I, ch. 3, section 6.

66   Walt Whitman, 'I Sit and Look Out', in *Leaves of Grass*

(London, Siegle Hill & Co., 1907), pp. 179–80.

67 Salah 'Abd al-Sabur, *Ma'sat al-Hallaj* (Cairo, 1965; English trans. Khalil I. Semaan, Leiden, Brill, 1972), Act 2, Sc. 2.

67 Hugo Grotius, *De Jure Belli et Pacis*.

68 Thomas Cranmer, The English Litany, in *The Book of Common Prayer*.

69 Shamsur Rahman, 'Poems of East Bengal', trans. Yusuf Jamal Begum, in *Presenting Pakistani Poetry*, op. cit., p. 88.

69 Ibn 'Abdus, 'Sword and Lance', in *Moorish Poetry*, trans. A. J. Arberry, op. cit., p. 63.

69 Prayer at the close of *Salat*.

69 Claude McKay, 'The Pagan Isms', in *Caribbean Voices*, vol. I: *Dreams and Visions*, op. cit., p. 100.

70 'Iyad Ibn Musa, 'Corn in the Wind', in *Moorish Poetry*, trans. A. J. Arberry, op. cit., p. 124.

70 Clement of Rome, *Epistle to the Corinthians*, LX–LXI, in *Opera Patrum Apostolicorum*, ed. F. X. Funk (Tübingen, 1887), vol. I, p. 134.

71 Anonymous, Somaliland, 'Camel-Watering Chant', trans. B. W. Andrzejewski and I. M. Lewis, in *Somali Poetry: An Introduction* (Oxford, Clarendon Press, 1964), p. 140.

71 Dag Hammarskjöld, *Markings*, op. cit., p. 123.

72 Zuhair, poet of the Jahiliyyah, *Mu'allaqah*, in C. J. Lyall, *Translations of Ancient Arabian Poetry* (2nd edition, London, Williams & Norgate, 1930), p. 113.

72 Anonymous, *The Banu Zimman*, poem of the Jahiliyyah, in C. J. Lyall, op. cit., p. 5.

72 Francis of Assisi.

72 Ibn al-Hajj, in *Moorish Poetry*, trans. A. J. Arberry, op. cit., p. 131.

73 W. B. Yeats, *Collected Poems* (London, Macmillan & Co., 1950), p. 288.

74 Muhammad al-Maghut, *The Postman's Fear*, trans. 'Abdullah al-Udhari, in *Modern Poetry of the Arab World*, (Harmondsworth, Penguin Books, 1986), p. 86.

74 Louis 'Awad, *Plutoland*, (Cairo, 1947), pp. 82–3.

75 Jalal al-Din Rumi, *Mathnawi*, trans. R. A. Nicholson

(London, Luzac & Co., 1925), vol. I, p. 180.

76 Eugène Ionesco, *Notes and Counter Notes*, trans. D. Watson (London, Calder, 1964), p. 160.

78 Josh Malihabadi, 'Our Society', trans. M. A. Seljuk, in *Presenting Pakistani Poetry*, ed. G. Allama, op. cit., p. 15.

78 Alexander A. Blok, in *Modern Russian Poetry*, trans. V. Markov and M. Sparks (London, MacGibbon & Kee, 1966), p. 179.

79 Francis Thompson, 'Orient Ode', in *The Collected Poetry* (London, Hodder & Stoughton, 1913), p. 148.

80 Balai of Aleppo, Syriac hymn for a church hallowing, in *Early Christian Prayers*, ed. Adalbert Hamman, op. cit., p. 187.

80 Abu Hamid al-Ghazali, *Al-Munqidh min al-Dalal*, final prayer (Cairo edition, AH 1309).

81 Muhammad Iqbal, *Javid Nama*, trans. A. J. Arberry (London, Allen & Unwin, 1966), lines 1061, 1063, 1064, 1066.

81 *Prayers of the Naqshabandi Order*.

82 Clement of Rome, *Epistle to the Corinthians*, LIX–LX, in *Opera Patrum Apostolicorum*, ed. F. X. Funk (Tübingen, 1887), vol. I, p. 134.

83 *Te Deum Laudamus* (conclusion), Morning Prayer, *Book of Common Prayer*.

83 Ahmad al-Tijani, *Prayers*.

84 Abu-l-'Ala al-Ma'ari, *Quatrains* XIV, XXIV, XXV, from *The Diwan of Abu-l-'Ala*, trans. Henry Baelin (London, John Murray, 1913).

84 'Abdul-Halim Josh, 'Let us forward go', trans. from Sindhi by G. Allama, in *Presenting Pakistani Poetry*, op. cit., p. 124.

85 Siraj of Andalusia, in *Moorish Poetry*, trans. A. J. Arberry, op. cit., p. 65.

85 Ibn Tufayl, concluding prayer in *Alive, Son of Alert*, ed. A. Amin (Cairo, 1952), p. 131.

85 Albert Camus, *The Plague*, trans. Stuart Gilbert (London, Penguin Books, 1960), p. 186.

86 Bertolt Brecht, 'Die Ausnahme und die Regel', in *Stücke*,

vol. V, ed. E. Burri and E. Hauptmann (Berlin, Suhrkamp, 1957), p. 187.

87 Stephen Crane, 'War is Kind', in *The Works of Stephen Crane*, op. cit., vol. VI, p. 131, no. XXII.

88 Aleksei K. Gastev, *Modern Russian Poetry*, trans. V. Markov and M. Sparks, op. cit., p. 699.

89 John Donne, 'Third Satire', in *Poetical Works*, ed. H. J. C. Grierson (Oxford, Clarendon Press, 1912), vol. I, p. 158, lines 100–2.

90 Ezra Pound, Canto XLV, *The Cantos of Ezra Pound* (London, Faber & Faber, 1964), pp. 239–40.

91 Thomas Traherne, *Centuries, Poems, and Thanksgiving*, op. cit., VI of *Christian Ethics*, pp. 187–8, lines 1, 10–11, 14–18, 19–21, 23–30.

92 Ezra Pound, 'Commission', in *Personae: Collected Shorter Poems* (London, Faber & Faber, 1952), pp. 97–8.

93 Richard Crashaw, 'To the Countess of Denbigh', in *Poems*, ed. A. R. Waller (Cambridge, Cambridge University Press, 1904), pp. 190–2.

94 Lancelot Andrewes, *Preces Privatae*, in *Lancelot Andrewes and his Private Devotions*, op. cit., pp. 99–103.

95 Ibn Hazm, *The Ring of the Dove*, op. cit., p. 181.

96 Kamel Hussein, *City of Wrong*, trans. Kenneth Cragg (Oxford, Oneworld Publications, 1994), p. 146.

97 Dennis Osadebay, from *West African Verse*, ed. D. I. Nwoga (London, Longmans, Green & Co., 1967) p. 15.

98 Shams al-Din Hafiz, 'Wild Deer', trans, A. J. Arberry in *Fifty Poems of Hafiz* (London, Cambridge University Press, 1947), p. 131.

98 Abu Hamid al-Ghazali, *The Reviving of Religion*, op. cit., p. 34.

100 Léopold Sédar Senghor, 'Night in Senegal', in *Selected Poems*, trans. John Reed and Clive Wake (London, Oxford University Press, 1964) p. 5.

100 Léopold Sédar Senghor, 'Prayer for Peace', in *Selected Poems*, op. cit., p. 51.

101 Jalal al-Din Rumi, *Mathnawi*, trans. R. A. Nicholson, op. cit., vol. I, lines 3069–73.

101 Walt Whitman, 'To Think of Time', in *Leaves of Grass*, op. cit., p.386.

102 Ezra Pound, 'Dieu! Qui L'a Faicte', in *Personae: Collected Shorter Poems*, op. cit., p. 84.

102 Abu-l-'Ala al-Ma'ari, *Letters of Abu-l-'Ala al-Ma'ari*, trans. D. S. Margoliouth (Oxford, Clarendon Press, 1898), no. 31, p.133.

103 Abu-l-'Ala al-Ma'ari, ibid, nos. 30, 35, 38 (2), and 41; pp. 132–3, 137, 140–1, and 144.

104 Gwendolyn Brooks, 'The Mother', in *Selected Poems*, (London, Harper & Row, 1962), p. 4.

106 George Campbell, 'Jamaica Constitution Day Poem', in *Caribbean Voices*, vol. I: *Dreams and Visions*, op. cit., p. 67.

107 Muhammad Iqbal, *Javid Nama*, op. cit., lines 1477–8.

107 George Campbell, 'Holy', in *Caribbean Voices*, vol. I: *Dreams and Visions*, op. cit., p. 94.

108 Michel Quoist, 'The Pornographic Magazine', in *Prayers of Life* (Dublin, Gill & Macmillan, 1965), p. 25.

109 Hilal Naji, *The Worshipper of the Flesh*.

109 Jalal al-Din Rumi, *Discourses*, trans. A. J. Arberry, op. cit., p. 28.

110 Michel Quoist, 'Eyes', in *Prayers of Life*, op. cit., pp. 35–7.

110 Shah 'Abdul Latif, 'Obstinate Eyes', trans. G. Allama, in *Presenting Pakistani Poetry*, op. cit., p. 104.

111 Alexander Pushkin, 'The Coach of Life', in *Poems from the Russian*, trans. F. Cornford and E. P. Salaman (London, Faber & Faber, 1943), p. 16.

112 Ezra Pound, 'The Return', in *Personae: Collected Shorter Poems*, op. cit., p. 85.

112 Ibn Hazm, *The Ring of the Dove*, trans. A. J. Arberry, op. cit., p. 174.

112 Karl Rahner, *Prayers for Meditation*, op. cit., p. 71.

113 *Corpus Inscriptionum Latinarum*, vol. II, p. 4964.

113 *Pilgrimage Prayers, Manasik al-Hajj wa Ad'iyat-al-Tawaf*, op. cit.

113 Egyptian Commendation, trans. by the editor from *Dictionnaire d'Archaeologie Chrétienne et de Liturgie* (ed. Cabrol et Leclercq), vol. XIV:1769.

113   *Monumenta Ecclesiae Liturgica*, trans. by the editor (ed. Cabrol et Leclercq), no. CXVIII.

114   Abu Hamid al-Ghazali, 'Morning Prayer of Abraham', in *The Reviving of Religion, Ihya 'Ulum al-Din*, op. cit., I, 9, p. 285.

114   Dag Hammarskjöld, *Markings*, op. cit., p. 93.

114   Ancient Irish Prayer, source unknown.

115   Søren Kierkegaard, *Journals*, op. cit., pp. 172–3.

115   Fakhr al-Din al-Razi, 'The Clear and the Shining', in *Muslim Devotions*, op. cit., pp.123–4.

INDEX OF AUTHORS
AND TITLES

INDEX OF THEMES
OF PRAYER

INDEX OF QURANIC PASSAGES

INDEX OF BIBLICAL PASSAGES